How to Plan Perfect Ki

Created and Designed by the Editorial Staff of Ortho Books

Project Editor
Jill Fox

Writer
Kathleen M. Kiely

Design Consultant
Jenepher Walker, CKD

Principal Photographer
Geoffrey Nilsen

Photography Editor
Roberta Spieckerman

Illustrator
Mitzi McCarthy

Ortho Books

Publisher
Robert B. Loperena

Editorial Director
Christine Jordan

Production Director
Ernie S. Tasaki

Managing Editors
Robert J. Beckstrom
Michael D. Smith
Sally W. Smith

System Manager
Linda M. Bouchard

Editorial Assistants
Joni Christiansen
Sally J. French

Address all inquiries to:
Ortho Books
Box 5006
San Ramon, CA 94583-0906

2 3 4 5 6 7 8 9
95 96 97 98 99

ISBN 0-89721-263-0
Library of Congress Catalog Card Number 93-86237

THE SOLARIS GROUP
2527 Camino Ramon
San Ramon, CA 94583-0906

Editorial Coordinator
Cass Dempsey

Copyeditor
Elizabeth von Radics

Proofreaders
Alicia K. Eckley
Fran Taylor

Indexer
Elinor Lindheimer

Editorial Assistant
John Parr

Layout by
Cynthia Putnam

Composition by
Laurie A. Steele

Production by
Indigo Design & Imaging

Separations by
Color Tech Corp.

Lithographed in the USA by
Banta Company

Kitchen Consultants
Beverly Wilson, CKD, Berkeley, Calif.; Dino Rachiele, ACSD, PKBP, Winstar, Apopka, Fla.; Doug Mattingly, Barrier Free Builders of Florida, Inc., Lakeland, Fla.

Special Thanks
AGA, Stowe, Vt.; Avonite, Inc., Los Angeles, Calif.; Azrock Industries, Inc.; Center for Independent Living, Berkeley, Calif.; City Cabinetmakers, San Francisco, Calif.; Contemporary Systems, Inc., Woburn, Mass.; Deborah Cowder; Bob Cox, The Guilds of Professional Cabinetry Space Planners, Baltimore, Md.; Mel and Shelly Freedman; Frigidaire Co., Dublin, Ohio; Linda and James Gerber; David and Marilyn Goodman; Chuck and Hilda Guzzetta; Henrik Hartz; Eric and Kaye Herbranson; Kitchenaid, Inc., St. Joseph, Mich.; Kitchen Services, Los Angeles, Calif.; Kitchen Works, San Francisco, Calif.; the Kostic family; Lamperti Associates, San Rafael, Calif.; Charles and Beverly McVay; Freddy and Neil Moran; National Kitchen and Bath Association, Hackettstown, N.J.; Sharon O'Connor and John M. Coreris, Jr.; Wm. Ohs Timeless Handmade Cabinetry; Rich Maid Kabinetry, Inc., Myerstown, Pa.; Nan and Tom Ryan; Sub-Zero Freezer Co., Inc., Madison, Wis.; Summitville Tiles, Inc., Summitville, Ohio; Tielsa/Wellman Kitchens; Dr. and Mrs. Hans Wilhelm.

Featured Kitchens
Special thanks to the following individuals and businesses for allowing us to photograph their work.
R = right, C = center, L = left, T = top, B = bottom

Carlene Anderson Kitchen Design, Oakland, Calif.: 1, 10, 16, 29, 52, 54, 66–67, 70, 72B, 91, 98
Barry Brukoff Design: 80T, 90
Coreris Cabinets and Construction, Emeryville, Calif.: 42–43, 49, 76
Judy Dawson, CKD, Hawaii: 80B, 86B
Charles Debbas Architecture: 62
Freedman and Freedman, Custom Cabinetry and Fine Woodworking, Emeryville, Calif.: 30, 80T, 82, 90
Linda Gerber Interior Design: 81B, 94
Harrell Remodeling, Inc., Menlo Park, Calif.: 51T, 51B, 63, 108
Jane Jackson and Associates, Architectural Drawings: 81B, 94
Gary Johnson, International Kitchen and Bath, Sunnyvale, Calif.: 4–5, 18, 19, 22–23, 58, 75TR, 95, 96
KitchenAid, Inc.: 99B
Paula McChezny, Barrier-Free Design/Color Consultant, San Mateo, Calif.: 13, 103T
Charlie and Lucy Metcalf, Designers & Builders: front cover, 54
Mueller-Nicholls Custom Cabinetry, Oakland, Calif.: front cover, 54, 70
Jane Phibbs, Designer: 26, 65
Nan Ryan with Special Thanks to Cañada College Teachers Carlene Anderson, CKD, Kathleen Claudon, CKD, and Jenepher Smith, CKD: 3, 93, 101B, 104–105

Photographers
Names of photographers are followed by the page numbers on which their work appears.
R = right, C = center, L = left, T = top, B = bottom.

AGA Cookers: 99T
Roger Hardy Photography, Menlo Park, Calif.: 51T, 51B, 63, 108
Muffy Kibbey Photography: front cover, 54, 70, back cover TL
Macario, Hawaii: 80B, 86B
James McNair: 72T
Geoffrey Nilsen Photography: 1, 3, 4–5, 10, 13, 16, 18, 19, 22–23, 26, 29, 30, 42–43, 49, 52, 58, 65, 66–67, 72B, 75TR, 76, 80T, 81B, 82, 90, 91, 93, 94, 95, 96, 98, 101B, 103T, 104–5, back cover TR & BR
Cesar Rubio Photography, San Francisco: 62
Widstrand Photography: 88, back cover BL

Front Cover
The serene balance of this dramatic space was achieved by planning every detail in harmony with all the other elements.

Title Page
The remodeling of this 1929 kitchen retained the French country theme of the house while meeting space requirements for modern appliances.

Page 3
The before and after floor plans for this kitchen are presented on pages 33 and 107.

Back Cover
Top left: The oak floor, brown-granite countertop, and stainless steel sink enhance the rich coloring of the pecan and walnut cabinets.
Top right: Abundant natural light, ample counter space, access to appliances, and convenient storage were high on the planning list for this kitchen.
Bottom left: This compact work center is as efficient as a ship's galley but versatile enough for the whole crew.
Bottom right: Cherry cabinets, slate flooring, and blue-green tiles create a rich blend of contrasting materials.

How to Plan Perfect Kitchens

PERSONALIZING YOUR KITCHEN

A beautiful and well-designed kitchen combines style and efficiency in a carefully planned space that is tailored to the people who use it. A kitchen remodel involves making decisions about improving the layout, increasing the capabilities of appliances, and improving the appearance of the room. After taking into consideration the structural features and limitations of the existing space, and the practical requirements of functional work centers, you'll find that the possibilities are limitless. Whether your present kitchen is the playground of a single chef or has to serve an army of individuals grabbing meals on the run, this chapter helps you determine its strengths and weaknesses. The discussion of popular styles and design theory will start you on your way toward realizing your dream kitchen.

Take the opportunity of planning your kitchen remodel to personalize the room and show off favorite items. Colors in the Oriental area rug are brought out by the granite countertop and backsplash tiles and the black door fixtures, drawer pulls, and sink accessories.

CHOOSING A KITCHEN LOOK

The right look for your kitchen balances your desired style with the elements of design theory. Use a unifying design concept when determining the colors, textures, patterns, line, and scale of the room configuration. Then use the same design concept when choosing the finishes, fixtures, appliances, and accessories that will fill it.

The Design Concept

Remodeling a kitchen involves making a number of choices, including many concerning the look of the room. This task is made easier by determining an overall design concept early in the process on which to base subsequent decisions. The design concept is composed of a style and a specific theme. A general overview of design theory makes the decisions easier (see page 7).

One of the first and most enjoyable steps in the remodeling process is gathering ideas and deciding what you want. Keep your eyes open as you visit other people's kitchens, peruse home-decorating magazines and books, and look at showroom displays. Tour model homes and historic houses and visit decorator and department-store showrooms to see different design elements in context.

Keep a clip file of your favorite ideas—an accordion file works well—and fill it with visual references, such as photographs, brochures, fabric swatches, and color samples. Don't worry about whether items go together at first; as the file grows, your personal sense of what you want will emerge.

Styles

Kitchen styles are divided into two broad classes: traditional and modern. Choosing the right style for your kitchen is a matter of personal preference and compatibility with the

Always consider the principles of design when establishing your kitchen look. The horizontal line of the counter and cabinet arrangement and smooth texture of polished wood, stainless steel, and solid-surface material define this kitchen as modern in style.

house. Traditional houses have wood windows, paneled doors, and intricate trim. Preserving the traditional style may eliminate the need to replace these items, saving time and money during construction, and ensures that the new kitchen complements the rest of the house. Modern houses feature metal windows, flush doors, and recessed lights, and staying with this style for the kitchen allows you to retain these fixtures.

Some people prefer that the entire home interior be of one style. If that is your preference, design the kitchen in accordance with the style of the rest of the house. Others, however, prefer the kitchen to be an oasis within the house; a cozy traditional kitchen can be a welcome retreat in a modern home. On the other hand, a sleek modern kitchen can be a refreshing change in an otherwise traditional house. If you choose an opposing style for the new kitchen, you can still coordinate it with the other rooms by using the same theme and by matching colors, patterns, and textures among areas of the house.

Traditional

A traditional-style kitchen has a refined air. The emphasis is on texture. Surfaces are of natural and timeless materials, such as wood, stone, and ceramic. Fixtures and furnishings show handcrafting and attention to detail. Lighting is subdued and directed, usually incandescent, and colors are muted.

Basic Design Theory

Create a sense of harmony in your new kitchen by incorporating basic design theory—line, scale, pattern, texture, and color—into your style and theme decisions. Weigh each of these as you develop the design, plan features, select fixtures, and choose finishes.

Line

The basic components of the kitchen—cabinets, counters, floor, and ceiling—form planes and edges that direct the eye, known as line. Long counters and a low ceiling form horizontal lines, considered modern. Tall, narrow cabinets and a high ceiling form vertical lines, which lend a traditional air. Manipulating line in design can disguise the basic shape of a room and change its ambiance.

Study the vertical and horizontal lines formed by features in the existing kitchen. Look for ways to smooth them out so that they align better with one another. You may not be able to move all the features into perfect alignment, but make as many adjustments as possible.

Cabinets with horizontal slats will elongate the room; vertical patterns will draw the eye upward. Inset panels on narrow doors tend to break up a horizontal look. A plain face on a cabinet will accentuate its edges and seams. Countertop edges that contrast with the cabinets create strong lines; countertops trimmed to match the cabinets mask the line. Determine the line you want to emphasize when drawing the floor plan, and then perpetuate it when selecting fixtures and choosing finishes.

Scale

An expression of relative size, scale refers to the relationships among the various elements of a room. A balance between the size of the room and the size of its components is most comfortable visually. A properly scaled space also relates well to the people using it.

A big kitchen can support large appliances, wide passageways, tall cabinets with raised-panel doors, bold-patterned wallcovering, and large floor tiles. A small kitchen requires proportionately smaller appliances, narrower cabinet doors with inset panels or flat faces, and more petite patterns on wallcoverings and flooring.

Pattern

The ordered regularity of the elements in a design is called the pattern. Examples are the design on wallpaper, the grid formed by ceramic tiles, and the shape of raised panels. Pattern gives a sense of movement. Many different patterns together look busy and tiresome, but too much of one pattern is overwhelming. However, some repetition of a pattern—such as a diamond-shaped counter repeated in the diamond tile accent on a backsplash and again in the window-treatment fabric—gives the room cohesion. Check accumulated patterns as they are inherent in materials, and can be created inadvertently when various materials are juxtaposed.

Texture

Everything has texture, both visual and tactile. In interior design, the visual texture of a material is as relevant as the way it feels. Most kitchens have smooth-textured surfaces for easy cleaning. Adding rough-textured accents, such as coarse-grain cabinet fronts, gives the kitchen a more natural, earthy feel.

Consider texture when choosing all your fixtures, as the same item may come in a choice of surface finishes. Matte texture tends to evoke a warm, traditional style, whereas glossy textures have a sleeker, more modern feel.

Color

While much of kitchen design involves rational decisions and verifiable measurements, the choice of color is personal and emotional. A powerful design element, color is a force in its own right that transforms space and gives it depth and character. To help make this rather major decision, consider the following rules of thumb for using color effectively. Dark or bold colors bring things closer and make a room feel smaller. Lighter tones make a room look more spacious, and cause objects to recede. Warm colors—red, orange, and yellow—are exciting and cozy. Cool colors—blue, green, and purple—are restful and passive.

Modern

Whether formal or homey, a modern-style kitchen has sleek, smooth surfaces and a clean-lined design. The emphasis is on horizontal lines and vivid colors—both high contrast and monochromatic. Materials are usually manufactured, such as laminate, stainless steel, glass, and chrome. Lighting is bright, usually fluorescent.

Themes

While the style defines the look of a room, the theme gives it personality. Certain combinations of materials, colors, and finishes evoke specific design themes. Combine the theme with the style to achieve the design concept you want for your kitchen. The theme serves as a common denominator among the individual aspects that appeal to you and is useful when describing what you want to suppliers.

Often, themes are vernacular, evoking a historical period or geographical reference. Consider a period theme if you live in a period house or like the style of a particular era. If you use the local geography as a regional theme, use local crafts to decorate the room.

A kitchen rarely falls into a single category that can be described in a few words, but the

Use of heavily textured materials, like the sugar pine cabinets, stone-tile floor, and ceramic-tile countertops of this kitchen, helps to define the traditional style. Vertical lines, exemplified here in the wood-slat backsplashes, are another feature of traditional styling.

list of descriptions that follows—which is by no means exhaustive—will give you some ideas and provide a vocabulary to work with as you develop a design theme.

Classic

Wood cabinets with furniture-quality design and finish, fine materials, and detailed appointments make a classic kitchen as elegant as any room in the house. Cabinets, doors, and windows are carefully trimmed with wood moldings, so select appliances that allow for matching wood-paneled fronts. Cabinets are framed with raised-panel designs and are built to the ceiling. Colors are natural yet sophisticated, and walls are usually papered. Natural materials, such as wood, ceramic tile, or stone, as well as fabricated materials in neutral colors, both project a classic look. Use old-world goods for accents, such as brass and copper for hoods, sinks, faucets, and lighting fixtures. Fine art and china and displayed brass or copper cookware are appropriate accessories.

Country

Less formal than the classic theme, the country kitchen evokes open-hearth cooking. In fact, a fireplace or wood-burning stove is the perfect focal point for the room. The atmosphere is warm and casual with an old-fashioned air. Display cooking utensils and dishes on open shelves and hang pots and pans from wall or ceiling racks. Bouquets of drying herbs and flowers or ropes of garlic, onions, or peppers add authenticity to the rustic feel of the room. Decorate with handmade linens and crafts.

Country kitchens allow for a vivid use of color. A triad scheme of basic yellow, red, and blue fits a country theme, as does a combination of blues and browns. Use rough textures in warm tones: cabinets that look like farmhouse furniture or old icebox doors, and countertops and backsplashes of ceramic tile—perhaps with hand-painted designs. Floors can be wood, ceramic tile, brick, or a resilient that mimics one of these materials; keep patterns simple in a small, repeated design.

A more rustic version of a country style—called Colonial—features wrought-iron accents and vertical raised panels on cabinet doors. The country theme can be modified to create various regional looks, with a New England or Southern emphasis, for example.

Eurotech

Featuring high efficiency in a small space, Eurotech kitchens are known for their streamlined, futuristic look and the marked absence of displayed items. This uncluttered, compact design is ideal for small kitchens. Plan a complementary color scheme using lots of white with bold accents in bright primary colors.

Cabinets are frameless with plain, flat doors of plastic laminate or wood veneer. Let the lines of the fixtures define any patterns, and keep textures sleek. Eurotech fixtures include brightly colored enameled faucets, white-wire shelving, and white, black, and primary-colored sinks in unusual shapes. Appliances are generally downsized, black or white, and often tucked out of sight or integrated into the cabinetwork. Although Eurotech fixtures and appliances were originally imported by European manufacturers, many American companies now produce items that fit this theme.

Accessorize with colorful, culinary accoutrements and modern art.

Art Deco

Its geometry softened by curved edges, this streamlined look arose early in the twentieth century as an expression of optimism for the fast-moving future. An American diner is a classic example of art deco in the kitchen. In the 1930s an architectural movement, called moderne, incorporated some features of art deco accentuated by angles rather than curves.

Metal is a basic material of both the art deco and moderne kitchen. Use metal cabinets and stainless steel countertops with chrome edges. Textures are sleek, with an occasional geometric relief, such as highly glazed tile backsplash in a daring zigzag or checkerboard pattern. Consider stacking trim

Metal cabinets are available in a wide range of colors allowing for a variety of moods. Cool blue cabinets evoke restfulness in this modern-style, Eurotech-theme kitchen.

three high at picture-molding height to accentuate the line of the room. In keeping with this theme, plan a high-contrast color scheme, such as black and white, accented with bright red, pink, or turquoise.

Gourmet

If you like the look of a restaurant kitchen, consider a gourmet theme. Beautiful for its stark utility, this no-nonsense kitchen is a serious cook's dream. A gourmet kitchen features commercial-style appliances that may include a commercial-style gas range, a huge hood, sub-zero refrigerator, and upright freezer. Spacious counters topped with marble, butcher block, ceramic, or stainless steel provide plenty of work space for true or aspiring chefs. Color is almost an afterthought in the gourmet kitchen, with industrial chrome accented by the food items and cooking wares on display. Accessorize the gourmet kitchen with the bare essentials: top-of-the-line pans, pots, and utensils, hung within reach from overhead racks for quick and easy access. Allow for plenty of storage space, including a pantry with heavy-duty metal shelves to accommodate specialty appliances, utensils, bulk foods, and cookbooks.

Period

Many people have an affinity for a particular historical period, perhaps to show off inherited or collected furnishings or artworks, to recreate a favorite historical site, or to match the kitchen theme to the architectural style of the house. With modern appliances, it is difficult to replicate exact periods—and who would want to reconstruct an outmoded kitchen devoid of modern conveniences?—but you can certainly provide a setting reminiscent of an earlier time. Consider tucking away modern appliances behind wood false fronts, using only finishes available during the chosen period, and installing window treatments and decorating accessories unique to that era.

Two remodeling goals of the owners of this kitchen were to replicate the kitchen of an English country cottage in which they had once lived and to have plenty of room to show off an antique china collection.

Regional

From current or past associations, family heritage, or travel, you may find a particular regional theme appealing. The theme may originate in the United States—New England, the Southwest, or the Northwest—or from a region of some other country—the south of France, rural Sweden, the English countryside, or industrial Japan. To evoke a region, use the materials and colors native to that area. When choosing finishes and fixtures, consider the type of wood and other materials used in the region. Find regional fabrics for window treatments, upholstery, and linens, and display authentic art and crafts to hone the theme.

Combining Colors

Harmonious color schemes can be created by combining colors from the color wheel in various ways. Choosing one or more intensities from the same segment produces a monochromatic scheme. Choosing colors from opposite sides of the wheel forms a complementary color scheme.

The Color Wheel

Color theory places colors in a continuum called the color wheel—an extremely useful tool for choosing a color scheme. It displays an inventory of basic colors, identifies the transition from color to color through the visual spectrum, and shows how colors are related to one another. The primary colors—red, blue, and yellow—are equally spaced. The secondary colors—orange, green, and purple—are placed between the two primaries that are its components. Completing the color wheel are the intermediate colors, mixtures of primary and secondary colors. These 12 full-strength colors are known as pure hues.

Because they are so intense, the colors of the color wheel are seldom used in their pure-hue forms except as accents. More often variations are created by adding a neutral color. When white is added to a color, a tint of that color is created. When black is added, a shade results. When gray is added, the result is a tone.

Neutrals—black, white, and gray—are not colors in the defined sense, yet they play a very important role in creating a balanced and varied color scheme. Use them for contrast, to soften a color scheme, or as an accent.

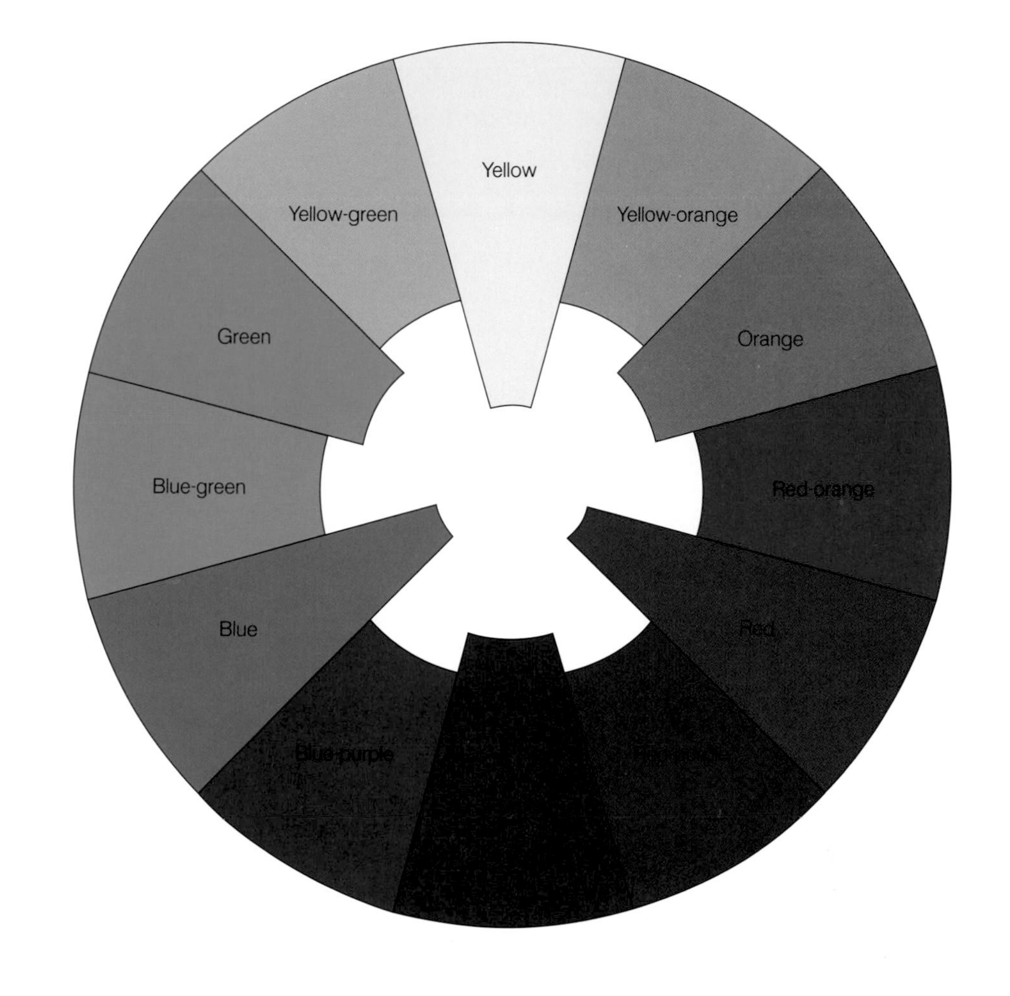

To produce a simple triad scheme, take colors from three segments spaced equidistantly. Another three-color scheme, called split complementary, is produced by taking one color from one segment and the other two colors from segments on each side of the segment opposite the first. Choosing colors from two or more contiguous segments creates an analogous, or related, color scheme. A quadratic scheme consists of colors from any four segments, so long as no two segments are adjacent.

Whichever method you use, remember that you will rarely use pure hues of the color wheel but rather relative values of those colors—that is, tints, shades, and tones. It is important to consider the relationship of lightness to darkness within your color selections, as well as the relationships among the colors themselves.

Colors in the Real World

Despite your preferences, you will find that the colors offered by manufacturers of kitchen appliances and fixtures follow strong design trends. However, if you stick to a color scheme that's uniquely yours, the kitchen will not look dated in a few years.

Where do you start? If there are permanent materials in the kitchen, start with that color and build a scheme around it, such as the color of a brick chimney or the colors in an adjacent room. Or, draw your inspiration from outside the realm of kitchen design: a favorite painting, a plate collection, a printed fabric, a custom tile, or the view from a window. Remember that all colors look far more intense on a large surface than in a tiny swatch or a photograph.

EVALUATING FAMILY NEEDS

Every family is unique. In order to create a kitchen that fits the way you live, you must identify the needs of each member. Involving the family at this early stage will broaden your perspective and increase everyone's enthusiasm for the big project.

Family Style

For the purposes of this book, the term *family* refers to the group of people living in the house. Remodeling a kitchen is a long-term investment in your home. The kitchen must suit your family as it changes over time. Now is the time to take an honest look at who you are as a family, so you can design a kitchen in which you will all feel comfortable.

Begin planning by making a list of everyone who uses the kitchen; consider all family members, their ages, and their needs as they relate to the kitchen. Include anyone who will use it, including frequent visitors and hired help. Is yours a combined family with different traditional uses for the kitchen?

Next, imagine as best you can the household 5 years from now and then 10 years from now. Is yours a family of adults? Do you anticipate any or more children? Will someone soon be leaving home? Will you eventually sell?

Number of Cooks

An essential figure to compute in your family survey is the number of people who will be cooking. The entire kitchen design is affected if the cooking is done by one person all the time, by several people at different times, or by multiple cooks working in the room simultaneously. With several cooks needing to move about the room at the same time, you need to provide space between major appliances, wider aisles—48 inches wide minimum for a two-cook kitchen—and more counter space: at least 2 extra feet per cook. You will also need more storage space for extra food-preparation tools, and more counter-level receptacles. You may even want to plan separate food-preparation areas, including multiple sinks, garbage disposers, and trash bins.

Various cooks will have different appliance preferences, which may affect choices in space requirements, power sources, and placement. The sooner the variations are recognized, the easier each preference will be to accommodate.

Special Needs

Many physical conditions once considered limitations are now viewed as human variations that can be compensated for in part by foresightful home design. When evaluating the family makeup, take into account members with special needs. Such needs vary, but all should be considered noteworthy, especially at this early stage in the planning process. List the needs of people who have restricted mobility or who use a walker or a wheelchair; are shorter or taller than average; have trouble reaching, bending, squatting, or grasping; or who have limited eyesight, color vision, or hearing.

Keep these special needs in mind as you develop the floor plan and choose fixtures and appliances. A kitchen designed

Multiple is the byword of this kitchen plan. Multiple cooking and cleanup centers allow several cooks to work simultaneously yet separately. A large family is accommodated by multiple appliances: two dishwashers, two trash compactors, two ovens, and a two-door, subzero refrigerator. Interior French doors to the laundry room provide multiple sources of natural light.

for a person with special needs can be comfortable for everyone. This concept is called universal design, or barrier-free building, and includes brighter lighting, wider doorways, and lowered counters. However, the design and planning principles outlined in this book are applicable no matter how the final design is realized.

Some special needs can be met simply by choosing carefully from normal, everyday fixtures and appliances. For example, if reach is a problem, consider lowering counters, installing burners in a single line along the counter edge, or installing a sprayer attachment to the sink for filling pots at various angles. Many kitchen-equipment manufacturers offer products with universal design. These include faucets with outsized lever handles, appliances with electronic touch pads, Braille appliance-control overlays, electric rotating shelving, and appliance use-and-care guides on audiotape.

Pets

List your fauna in the family survey as well. If your dog, cat, or pot-bellied pig is part of the family, you'll need storage space in the kitchen for its food and other supplies. Consider an out-of-the-way spot for food and water bowls; a warm place for a bed; a grooming area; and pet-door access, as applicable. Most floor materials can sustain the extra traffic of four-legged family members, although you should keep in mind potential scratches on wood floors and the sound of pet nails on hard surfaces, such as ceramic and stone tiles.

A wheelchair user remodeled this galley-shaped condominium kitchen to serve his special needs. The open space under the cooktop allows him to pull in close while cooking; shelves in the opening hold pots and pans; burner controls are placed within reach on the right side of the cooktop. Eliminating the under-sink cabinet and lowering the counter provide sink access.

DETERMINING KITCHEN ACTIVITIES

Once you've figured out who will use the kitchen, you need to determine what each person will do there. First, analyze what each family member does in the kitchen and how the present design helps or hinders the activity. Next, imagine uses you want to add to the kitchen during remodeling.

Food Preparation

Whatever else the kitchen may be used for, its primary function is as the food-preparation center. Begin by evaluating how your family prepares meals and how the process can be made easier by a better kitchen design. List the needs for every meal, including weekday breakfasts, weekend brunches, lunches, family dinners, and cooking for guests. Consider each type of meal, the time you'd like to spend preparing it, the number of cooks, and the cooking preferences of each.

Tour the existing kitchen, going through the motions of meal preparation; note what you like and dislike about the process. For most people, one or two major problems pop to mind immediately—probably the reasons that compelled you to remodel in the first place. Jot these down, and then think about smaller details, both positive and negative, that affect food-preparation ease and enjoyment.

Room Layout

The first consideration is the general layout of the room, including traffic patterns, the distance between appliances, and the way opening doors interact. Perhaps you find yourself running back and forth to fetch

Spacious food-preparation centers, plenty of storage space, a casual eating area, and a home office were all planned into this square-shaped kitchen by designing a two-tiered peninsula as a room inside a room. Sleek, solid-surface-material countertops, laminate drawer and cabinet doors, and scrubbable wallcoverings allow for quick cleanup of even this large space.

utensils or food, or bumping into someone crossing the room while you're working at the stove. If so, note it. Also consider the quality of lighting and ventilation and how they help or hinder the cooking experience.

Space

Elbow room is the second consideration. As you cook, are you cramped by a lack or inefficient use of space? Cooking in even very small kitchens can be quite comfortable if everything is arranged well. Is there adequate room for all the major and minor appliances? Is there sufficient space for utensils and food, including cost-saving bulk storage? Is there enough counter space for various cooking activities?

View the countertops as a workbench for the kitchen. Is there sufficient surface area—width and depth—on which to work? As you prepare a meal, think of where you'd prefer to set a dish, chop a vegetable, or roll out dough. How much space do you need for each activity? In general, you need counter space at the range, the sink, the refrigerator, and the microwave oven. It is also handy to have a clean surface near the door for depositing grocery bags.

Also check that the counters are at a convenient height for everyone who uses them. Consider counters at several levels for different activities and different cooks. While contemplating the countertops, decide whether you like the present material. How easy is it to keep clean? Do you like the color and texture? Has it worn well? Would you like special countertops of stone, butcher block, or stainless steel for certain kitchen activities?

Power Sources

Evaluating the power sources for cooking is the next priority. Survey the sources in the existing room—gas, electric, or both. Which source do you prefer? Is the existing range, stove, or cooktop gas or electric? If you favor one fuel source over another, your remodeling plan should reflect that preference.

Appliances

Next, evaluate the major appliances. List those you'd like to add to the new kitchen, then list the existing appliances and ask yourself whether you are satisfied with the performance of each. How old is it? Is it energy efficient? Is the noise level acceptable? Most appliances last many years, and not replacing them needlessly when remodeling can save a lot of money.

Examine each cooking appliance, bearing in mind how each cook prefers to work. Does the cooktop have enough burners? Are they placed conveniently? Do they get hot enough? Would you like to add a grill, griddle, wok, or rotisserie? Do you have enough ovens? Are they large enough? Is it essential that they be self-cleaning? Do you have a convection oven? A microwave? Is it big enough? Powerful enough? Do you need more than one?

Now evaluate the refrigerator and freezer. Is the location convenient? Does it block your light, break up an expanse of counter, or stop traffic? It can be placed out of the food-preparation area to allow for more counter space. If you decide to move it, is the door reversible? Next check the refrigerator and freezer capacities. Is the refrigerator the right size? One that is too large runs inefficiently. Does the door seal need replacing? Is the interior conveniently designed? Do you prefer a different style: a side-by-side, or a model with the freezer on the bottom? Do you want a streamlined, 24-inch-deep model that fits flush with the cabinets? Is the freezer large enough? Is it frost-free? Does it have an ice maker, or can one be added? This will require additional plumbing. If you use a lot of frozen foods, do you need a separate freezer located in the kitchen?

Be sure to consider the looks of existing appliances. Do they match each other and will they fit into the design concept? If the major appliances are sound, consider cosmetic sprucing—new handles or chrome, refinished enamel, decorative front panels—to rejuvenate them. If you plan to replace an existing appliance eventually, make sure the space it occupies will accommodate the new model.

Now list the minor appliances you use or hope to use in the future. Labor-saving devices aren't doing their job if they are awkward to store or take up valuable counter space. Which small appliances do you use every day: toaster oven, blender, food processor, coffee grinder, coffeemaker? Do they have a permanent space on the countertop or convenient storage? Where do you keep appliances you use occasionally: mixer, breadmaker, electric knife? Can you do without any of them? Do you plan to invest in any more? Would you prefer them on display or stored away? Are the electrical receptacles conveniently located? Do you have enough receptacles—and enough power—to run several machines at once?

Storage

The need for more storage space is often a main reason for remodeling a kitchen. To determine your needs, calculate the storage requirements for all the activities you perform—or want to perform—in the kitchen and the amount of space desired for each. Your list may range from storing flatware and canned goods to a popcorn maker and pet food.

Next, measure the amount and type of storage in the existing kitchen. Is there enough? Is it in the form you want? For example, do you prefer drawers rather than shelves? Do you want open or closed storage? Is there a pantry? Is there space in an adjoining room that you can break into to create one? Would you rather use existing storage space to expand the kitchen?

Also consider the quality of the existing storage. What is the condition of the cabinets? Are they the right size and configuration? Is there wasted space, such as blind-corner cabinets and closed soffits? Are the shelves awkward or difficult to reach? Do you like the surface material, the color, the handles?

As you inspect the existing storage, determine whether everything currently stored in the kitchen needs to be stored there, then ruthlessly discard items that you don't use, and move those that can be stored elsewhere.

Eating Areas

Providing a comfortable place for your family to share meals should be another goal of kitchen remodeling. Consider whether the existing kitchen allows you to dine in the style you prefer or if its design is dictating how you eat.

Specifically, determine how many people will eat together

Storage space needn't be totally hidden. In this cleverly designed kitchen, an open area above the cabinets provides room for a whimsical pitcher collection. Glass doors (pictured open) allow visual access to the pantry at all times. Open, recessed shelves show off serving platters. Behind the chair at left, wooden dowels provide a handy hanging rack for newspapers and magazines.

for which meals; include everyone in the family and frequent guests, keeping in mind children's ages and eating habits.

Next, contemplate the style in which you prefer to eat. Are the views you see during mealtimes enjoyable and conducive to relaxation? Is there a pleasant landscape a dining area could overlook? Some people like a kitchen atmosphere when eating, whereas others loathe seeing the sink while they dine.

If your present meal accommodations are awkward, what arrangements would work better? Is there a snack counter, breakfast nook, or dining area in the kitchen? How much use does it get? How convenient is it? Is it out of the way of traffic? Is the lighting adequate? Do you want to encourage eating in the kitchen? You may want different eating areas for different meals.

When computing space, be sure to figure in the seating as well; bench seating built into one or more walls can save space. Also think about the traffic flow between food-preparation and eating centers. Is there enough room for placing all the food within reach of the diners? Is there adequate storage for table linens, flatware, and dishes near each eating area?

Entertaining

It seems that no matter how small the kitchen or how formal the party, everyone always ends up in the kitchen. As you evaluate family activities, consider how often you entertain, your style of entertaining, and the number of guests you usually invite over. Then reflect on how your existing kitchen meets these needs.

Entertaining requires extra space for food preparation and display, beverage service, and areas for eating and visiting. The amount of space needed depends on how you entertain.

If you cook meals for large groups often, consider installing extra appliances to handle the load, such as a second dishwasher, sink, or refrigerator; additional cooktop burners; or another oven.

If you prefer to entertain formally, figure the needs of hired help and the convenience of transferring food from the kitchen to the dining room. If the existing kitchen has an open plan, you may want to add a partition wall to block the view between the food-preparation and dining centers.

If you entertain casually, the kitchen is probably the center of activity. Does traffic flow easily from the kitchen to the living area and the backyard? If not, consider taking out walls to create an open-plan kitchen. If you'd prefer less party traffic while you cook, consider adding a wet bar with a small refrigerator to another room. To make it fun for guests to help in the kitchen, consider a large island or peninsula, where all can gather to slice, dice, and trade stories.

Cleanup

A well-planned kitchen makes cleanup quick, easy, and efficient. Cleanup includes dishwashing, disposing of food waste and trash, and storing materials for recycling. Consider ways each of these activities could be improved if handled differently.

Dishwashing

Determine the ways you wash dishes now. Is the space adequate and the setup comfortable? Is the cleanup center convenient to the eating center? Are you pleased with the location, look, and configuration of the sink? Do you prefer one sink or two? Even if you have a dishwasher, you still need some drainage area. Is there enough counter space for stacking dirty dishes and draining clean ones?

If there is a dishwasher in the existing kitchen, you need to evaluate its efficiency and suitability for the new kitchen before deciding to replace it. You also need to determine if the location and relationship to the sink are adequate. Is it convenient to load and unload? Is there room to stand at the sink when the door is down? Is it too noisy?

Waste Disposal

There are several methods available for cleaning up food waste. Determine how you prefer to deal with this necessity, check the existing system, and plan ways that the new kitchen design can accommodate your preferred method.

If you have a disposer now, you'll probably want to retain it, and it can be moved if you are moving a sink. If you do not have a disposer now and plan to purchase one, check local codes first. Some codes—especially those pertaining to septic systems—disallow disposers.

Trash Disposal

Garbage is a reality, but not all trash should be tossed away; storage for recycling should be a part of any new kitchen design. What method do you have in the existing kitchen for collecting trash? Is it hidden or out in the open? Food-preparation, cleanup, and home-office areas each produce different types of garbage. Plan a collection point near each activity center for trash and recyclables.

If you have a trash compactor but it gets little use, would the extra cabinet space be more valuable to you?

Laundry

Because the kitchen may already contain the plumbing and power sources necessary for a washing machine and clothes dryer, it may be a convenient place to locate the laundry center. A laundry center requires hot and cold water, special electrical receptacles, and possibly, in the case of a gas dryer, a gas line.

If you are contemplating moving the laundry to the kitchen, determine the plumbing and electrical needs; the space requirements for the machines, laundry products, and dirty clothes; and the need for a folding area. Keep in mind the noise of the machines in action and how that may affect other kitchen activities.

If the laundry is already located in the kitchen, determine if the machines are in the ideal configuration to fit the space and whether they will be replaced. Laundry machines are available in side-by-side and stacked models in a range of sizes. Front-loaders can be concealed within counters as well as in closets.

Besides the machines and storage space, a laundry center might also include a place for an ironing board and supplies, or perhaps a sewing area.

Communications

In many households, the kitchen invariably is the communications center for the whole family: where members congregate for conversation or help with homework; where mail and messages are left and retrieved; and where the family calendar is located—right next to the telephone. If this sounds familiar—or attractive—to you, a dual role as "communications central" may be ideal for your new kitchen. Evaluate your space requirements for a home office and a homework and hobby area, and wiring for communication and media facilities.

Home Office

A central location for leaving mail, messages, and notes prevents many communication mix-ups in a busy family. A home office can range from a small space to pay bills to an area large enough to conduct a home-based business.

Consider how you want to use the office. Will you use it to chat on the telephone, pay bills, or conduct business? Is this to be a quiet work space or merely a place to store paperwork? Do you need bookshelves, a file drawer, a bulletin board? List the business machines you'd use, including perhaps a telephone, answering machine, calculator, fax machine, computer, and printer. All these machines, plus the lighting source, require individual wiring and receptacles. Estimate the amount of space needed for these items, as well as desk space and a chair.

Hobbies and Homework

If you have a hobby—such as crafts, sewing, potting plants, or game playing—that you'd like to pursue in the kitchen, determine its space, storage, receptacle, and lighting needs, then decide if the new kitchen is an appropriate location.

If the children do homework and school projects in the kitchen, consider a durable counter, at table height, with plenty of lighting and storage for their supplies.

Media

If your family will be participating in many activities in the kitchen, do you want to listen to music or watch television while there? Remodeling is an opportunity to install hidden stereo wire, speakers, and TV cable.

Laundry appliances can be incorporated into a kitchen without their utilitarian nature overwhelming the space. To the left of the stacking washer and clothes dryer is an ironing board cabinet.

If television watching is on your family's wish list, consider where you most want to watch it, and then look around for a usable space to locate it. Here an unused chimney near the eating area provides a perfect place for table-linen storage, an extra oven, and a slide-out television. The opposite wall of this kitchen is pictured on page 4.

UNDERSTANDING THE EXISTING STRUCTURE

Striking a workable balance between what you have and what you want is the challenge of remodeling. The house structure—its existing floor plan, age, architectural style, and the quality of its construction—greatly affects the complexity and cost of the remodeling project.

Reviewing Existing Plans

The easiest way to understand your house structure is to obtain a copy of the original plans. If you do not have them in your files, contact the builder, architect, mortgage holder, or county building department. If you live in a neighborhood of tract homes, ask neighbors if they have their house plans, which will be similar to yours. The plans will indicate the type of construction and placement of utility systems throughout the house.

If you cannot locate the plans, you must do some research and a physical inspection to learn exactly how your house is built. Even if you find the plans, you should still conduct a physical inspection to check the structure for soundness and aesthetic factors; look at each room from a construction as well as an appearance point of view. Is there peeling paint or water damage? Is there an architectural feature, such as high ceilings or a fireplace, to use to advantage? Also assess whether any remodeling has been done over the years. Was the existing kitchen remodeled? Have the electrical or plumbing systems been upgraded? Have structural changes been made? Make note of these on the plans.

House Age

Building methods and materials have changed over the years, for the most part becoming simpler, lighter, and more standardized, and thus facilitating remodeling. The more the home predates modern construction standards, the more complicated the remodeling.

Older homes often do not meet current building codes; remodeling the kitchen may involve mandatory upgrading of certain structural factors and utility systems. Be sure to consult your local building department prior to finalizing your kitchen design.

House Style

Carefully study the interior and exterior style of the house and how it relates to the kitchen. Identify the style in which the house was built and the interior design concept. If you want a cohesive look to the entire house, the kitchen remodel will have a definite design concept to fit the overall style.

Room Style

Next, reflect on the existing kitchen style and theme. Are you satisfied, or is a tired look one of the reasons you're remodeling? Assess the quality, material, and color of various fixtures and features. Are they inviting or off-putting? Easy or difficult to maintain? Make note of specific features you are comfortable with and those features that are daily annoyances.

Room Placement

Evaluate the position of the kitchen in relation to the rest of the house, noting adjoining rooms and uses, including stairways and closets. Can some of this space be annexed for the new kitchen? Check access in and around the kitchen, observing traffic patterns through the room and any places where gridlock occurs. Does the family use the kitchen as a hallway to get to the dining room, backyard, or garage? Do you have a kitchen to which everyone gravitates, or is it removed from daily activities? Do you like it that way?

Go outside and observe the immediate surroundings. Are the indoors and outdoors integrated? Are attractive views being exploited? Do you carry foods outdoors? Is there room to expand the kitchen?

Views

Among the many visual aspects in a room are looking out from within, looking in from without, and looking around within the room itself. Stand at various points in the kitchen and survey your surroundings. What do you see while washing the dishes, while sitting at the table, and while working at the counter? Do you like what you see? If there is nothing remarkable within the room, speculate on ways to create a pleasant view. Is there a space in the kitchen you'd like to feature—to make a visual focal point—by adding a window, installing shelves for displaying collections, or hanging artwork?

What view do you have from the kitchen windows and open doors? Do you see children playing in the yard, a tree or garden, or the compost bin? Imagine ways to change the kitchen that would eliminate poor views and capitalize on more worthwhile scenery. Is it possible to open up a wall to gain a view?

Also look toward the kitchen from various points in the house. Can you see the sink from the front door? Is this the first impression you want guests to have? Observe the rooms that open into the kitchen and how the kitchen looks from them.

Construction Method

Ascertain as much as you can about the hidden construction elements of the home. Note the construction method and materials used for walls, floors, and ceilings. Check the type and quality of electrical, plumbing, heating, cooling, and ventilating systems. The house plans should contain most of the pertinent information, but an inspection of the house will reveal any changes, the quality of materials, and any problems that need repair. If neighbors with a similar home have remodeled, ask what construction details they discovered during their project.

Structural Survey

Use the existing floor plan and a physical inspection of the house to reach a thorough understanding of the existing structure. Keep your eyes wide open as you inspect the house; it is vital that you determine everything that needs to be considered, improved, or adjusted. You can prioritize the needs list later, as you develop the floor plans and itemize the budget.

Walls

What is the frame construction method?
How high are the walls from floor to ceiling?
Which walls are load-bearing?
How thick are the walls?
What is the stud size?
What is the spacing of studs, center to center?
What is the wall substrate?
What is the finish treatment?
How are the walls trimmed?
Rate the condition of each wall.

Floor

What is the type of structural floor?
Is the space below the floor easily accessible?
What is the finish floor treatment?
How is the floor edged?
Rate the condition of the baseboards, thresholds, and floor.

Ceiling

What is the configuration of the ceiling (flat or sloped)?
In what direction do ceiling joists run?
What is the spacing of joists, center to center?
Is the insulation satisfactory?
How is the ceiling finished?
Rate the condition of the ceiling.

Doors

List the number of doors that access the kitchen.
Is the width of each door adequate?
Is the swing direction of each door appropriate?
Indicate the style and material of each door.
How is each door trimmed?
Rate the condition of each door and frame.

Windows

List the number of windows in the kitchen.
Does the window/skylight area equal at least 10 percent of the kitchen floor area (or larger living space if the kitchen is included)?
How is the view from each window? Are there better views?
Is any window oriented well for a greenhouse or bay window?
Indicate the style, material, and condition of each window.
How is each window trimmed?
Are the windows well insulated?

Electrical

What is the breaker rating supporting the kitchen?
- Number of breakers?
- Amperage of each?

Is the electrical service adequate?
List the number, type, and location of receptacles.
- Where are appliance receptacles?
- Which are 120 volt?
- Which are 240 volt?
- Which are grounded?
- Are receptacles in wet areas (next to sinks) protected by ground fault circuit interrupters (GFCI)?

Where are the lighting fixtures located?
List the number and types of fixtures.
Is lighting fluorescent or incandescent?
Where are the light switches?
Are the switches conveniently located?
Rate the quality of the lighting.
- How is the light for specific tasks?
- How is the overall ambiance?

Plumbing

What are the pipes made of?
Where are drainpipes vented?
Are appliances plumbed adequately?
- Washing machine?
- Dishwasher?
- Ice maker within the refrigerator?

Do the pipes knock?
How is the water pressure?
Is there evidence of rust in the water?
Does the sink drain well?
Indicate the location, capacity, and quality of the water heater.
Is there gas service to the existing kitchen?

Ventilation

How is the kitchen heated and cooled?
Note the location of heating and cooling outlets.
Are there places to incorporate solar heating and cooling techniques?
How is the cooktop vented?
Where does the vent pass to the outside?
Is the ventilation adequate year-round?

HERBS

DESIGNING THE SPACE

Once you have a thorough understanding of your existing kitchen and some specific ideas of what you want from the new one, the next step is to put the two together in a design that is beautiful, functional, and fits the space. Time spent trying out various designs on paper to arrive at the best possible plan before beginning construction is well invested. This chapter presents ways to add space to a room and to organize kitchen elements into practical work centers. These processes are based on tried-and-true research and use professional drafting techniques.

Every surface—walls, ceiling and floor—must be considered when designing a room. In this kitchen a desire for more light meant changing the outside wall by adding an angled bay window and changing the ceiling by adding a skylight. There is another view of this kitchen on page 18.

ADDING SPACE TO THE KITCHEN

When evaluating your family's many kitchen activities, you may have concluded that the existing space just isn't big enough. This problem is not insurmountable; by looking around with a creative eye, you'll find adding space to the existing kitchen can be quite simple.

Using Space Effectively

There are many methods of acquiring additional space without adding actual square footage to the kitchen. The most basic is ensuring that you store in your kitchen only those items and appliances you actually use. Selling redundant items at a garage sale or donating them to charity may be your most effective means to gaining extra kitchen space.

Within the kitchen proper, consider the simplest options first. If there are any odd jogs in the walls, examine them—they may cover an unused flue chase, ventilation duct, or old chimney. By removing the finish wall you can gain several feet of storage space or just the nook you need for the home-office desk.

Assess the spaces between studs for smaller storage areas. Although sixteen inches wide and four inches deep doesn't sound like much, it's an ideal space for a spice rack or collection display.

Check your traffic patterns. You can add several feet of floor space by closing off an unused door or unnecessary window.

Adding Windows

A brighter room feels larger. If the kitchen seems dark or cramped, add a window. Greenhouse and bay windows incorporate space from outside without a major structural change to the house. In addition, a greenhouse window provides shelf space, and a bay window can add floor or seating space, especially useful as a breakfast nook.

By flooding a kitchen with light and establishing a high visual focal point, skylight windows give the illusion of space. Skylight kits are designed to fit between standard rafters, and installing them does not require a huge amount of construction expertise.

Another way to bring the outside in is to install sliding glass or French doors opening onto a patio, deck, or porch. To link the indoor and outdoor spaces, finish the two floorings similarly.

Raising the Ceiling

Rooms can be expanded up as well as out. If the kitchen has a suspended ceiling, such as a grid of translucent light panels, removing them will expose the ceiling. If the roof or an attic is directly over the kitchen, you can take down the ceiling and cut out any joists to create a vaulted ceiling open all the way to the roof rafters.

Adding Square Footage

A more complicated method of adding space to the kitchen is to go beyond the walls of the existing room. You can do this by expanding into an adjoining room, or by moving an exterior wall, thereby actually adding square footage to the house.

Moving Interior Walls

If adding kitchen space is a priority, consider nearby rooms that can be sacrificed for the cause. The simplest ways to expand the space visually are to cut a pass-through in an interior wall or widen a doorway and raise it to the ceiling. To physically enlarge the kitchen, do a little sleuthing to discover underused space on the other side of the walls. Older homes were often designed as a network of small rooms with distinct functions and often include a utility room off the kitchen. As appliances have changed, this room may have been relegated to storage. Would the space be better utilized as part of the working kitchen? Your house may have a formal dining room near the kitchen; does your family use it? Would you be better served by incorporating the space into the kitchen?

Next consider annexing all or part of an adjoining living area to add to the kitchen. You needn't take over the entire space; perhaps moving walls just a few feet into an adjacent room would gain desired square footage. How much do you need that closet or bathroom just off the kitchen? Check the often-idle space beneath stairs for locating storage or a specific appliance.

Load-Bearing Walls

The most critical consideration in removing a wall or adding a door, window, or pass-through is whether the wall bears the load in supporting the house structure. Assume that all exterior walls are load-bearing.

Interior walls that run perpendicular to the joists are often load-bearing as well. If a wall runs the entire length of the house, with few doors, or there is a wall upstairs and downstairs in the same position, chances are it is load-bearing.

If you alter a bearing wall, you must install a ceiling beam or a post to assume its load. Nonbearing walls may be removed as you wish, without affecting the house structure. If you have any doubts, consult a professional before making your plans.

Before any wall can be removed or altered, the utilities within it—wiring, plumbing, and ducting—must be disconnected and their alternate routing determined.

Legalities

As soon as you've decided to remodel the kitchen, pay a visit to the local building department to find out the building codes that pertain to the job and how to obtain the necessary permits. Codes vary by locality, so be sure you get correct, firsthand information. Codes that might affect a kitchen remodel include building, plumbing, mechanical, and electrical codes. There may also be additional state and local codes, most of which conform to—but may also contradict and override—the national model codes. Get up-to-date copies of all codes—condensed versions will do—and study them.

Neighborhood homeowners' associations may also have covenants that restrict the changes you can make to your house. Also peruse your deed for any restrictions on the use of the property.

Permits

In general, cosmetic changes and routine maintenance may be performed without a permit. These include removing cabinets, laying floor covering, installing a new countertop, and replacing a door or a window. But any job that affects the structure of the house or its utilities is regulated. You will need one or more permits to do structural work. Permits ensure that the work on your house—and nearby houses—is being done according to codes determined best for the public safety. Remodeling done without required permits can result in problems obtaining homeowner's insurance or selling the house. In some areas, you are allowed to do only the most minor plumbing or electrical jobs; a licensed plumber or electrician will have to apply for the permits and do the bulk of the work.

Ask the following questions before you start the permit process.

- What permits are necessary for the project?
- What must you present to apply for each permit?
- What are the permit fees?
- How long is the typical wait between application and approval?
- When will inspections be made?

Zoning

A kitchen remodel that will change the size or exterior appearance of the house may be controlled by zoning regulations. Zoning protects the character and quality of a neighborhood. If your plans conflict with zoning regulations, you can apply for a variance; a hearing may be necessary. The decision is made by the local planning board. It may regulate some of the following construction aspects.

- Architectural style: This may affect the type of siding, the roof style, the size and style of windows and doors, and the compatibility of the addition with the style of the house.
- Setback: This is the minimum distance between a building and the property line. You must know the exact boundaries of your property. A second story must sometimes be set back farther than the ground floor.
- Height: Some regulations restrict second-story additions. If you are considering expanding the kitchen, check that you can do so both structurally and legally.
- Parking: If enclosed off-street parking is required, you may not be able to expand the kitchen into the garage.

Moving Exterior Walls

If you cannot expand enough within the house, explore going outside. If a porch or patio is adjacent to the kitchen, consider enclosing it or attaching a prefabricated greenhouse, either of which would add usable space to the kitchen.

An exterior wall can be extended 2 or 3 feet by cantilevering the floor joists out from the foundation, eliminating the need to add to the house foundation. Additions greater than 3 feet require the construction of additional foundation piers. In either case you must consider the continuation of the roof line or construction of a new roof.

Additional costs include the foundation and wall construction materials, including framing lumber, exterior siding, insulation, doors, windows, interior wallboard, and subflooring. If you are expanding onto a porch, you may have to build up the porch floor to make it level with the interior floor, and augment the walls and foundation to bring them up to code for interior construction. In addition, you will be faced with zoning laws concerning exterior changes to the house and minimum setbacks.

If you must have a bigger kitchen and you cannot expand the existing space satisfactorily, you can move the kitchen to a different area of the house or add a new room entirely. While both of these options involve major construction, the design and planning stages remain the same. An advantage of this idea is that you can continue using the current kitchen as you build the new one.

ORGANIZING THE FUNCTIONAL AREAS

Since the 1950s, researchers have been developing standards for kitchen design, modifying them as family life changes. Your new kitchen can benefit from the very latest design principles, detailed here.

Standard Practices

The elements that make up the kitchen must fit together harmoniously so that movement within the kitchen is efficient and unimpeded. Basic kitchen design has for decades organized space into three work centers, with their relationship forming a work triangle around which traffic flow is diverted. The triangle is based on a study done at Cornell University for the Small Homes Council in the 1950s. Since then, dramatic life-style changes—two-career families, multiple cooks, labor-saving appliances, and recycling, to name a few—have altered the role of the kitchen. Seeing the need for standards that would take kitchen design into the twenty-first century, the National Kitchen and Bath Association recently asked experts at the University of Minnesota to reevaluate the Cornell standards. The new NKBA–Minnesota standards provide for the multiple-cook kitchen, the kitchen as a family activity center, and the proliferation of modern appliances. This section incorporates these latest standards.

One of the primary work centers of every kitchen is dedicated to cooking. Here, a component system is made up of a separate cooktop with storage beneath, an under-counter oven, and a grill. Plan flame-resistant surface treatments, such as this white ceramic tile, on either side of each cooking appliance to use for setting down hot foods.

Design Professionals

If the desired changes in your kitchen are complex, or your confidence in your design skills is limited, consider seeking the help of a design professional.

Qualified kitchen designers have the initials *CKD*—for Certified Kitchen Designer—listed after their names. This signifies that the person has passed rigorous written and design tests through the National Kitchen and Bath Association. Kitchen designers work independently, in association with architects and builders, or are allied with retail dealers.

There are a number of ways to find a kitchen designer. Ask people who have remodeled their kitchen for recommendations. Track down the firm or individual designer who worked on a kitchen featured in the local press. Check out the designers who have worked on nearby showcase and model homes. If you have worked with an interior designer, ask for recommendations of qualified kitchen designers. If your plans include an extensive addition to the house as well as a kitchen remodel, you may want to pursue the overall design through an architect, who may have a kitchen designer on staff. If you plan to hire a contractor, ask him or her for referrals. Stop by local building-supply outlets and cabinet showrooms, or let your fingers do the walking through the telephone directory. Many kitchen-supply retailers employ certified designers, whose services often come gratis with major purchases.

Finding a kitchen designer who is right for your job is much like seeking the right dentist, doctor, or other professional. Much is contingent on rapport and your respect for the designer's experience, taste, and specialized knowledge. Ask to speak to former customers and visit completed jobs, if possible, to view a designer's work before making any commitments.

The better the designer understands what you want, the more likely he or she will produce the perfect kitchen for you. When meeting with a kitchen designer initially, bring your wish list, your clip file of favorite looks, the survey of the existing structure, your preliminary plans, and your budget requirements.

Kitchen designers can be fairly flexible in their role, which can include checking that the plan you designed is workable, providing a complete floor plan, or overseeing the entire remodeling job. Whatever best suits your time and your budget, as well as the designer's schedule, should determine how active a role the designer will play in your remodeling project.

Work Centers

The NKBA–Minnesota study designates primary and secondary work centers. A work center is the spot where a major kitchen activity is focused. Your kitchen must include the primary work centers, and may include the secondary work centers as needed.

Each work center has a suggested minimum countertop space, which is measured along the front edge, called the countertop frontage. The surface area at an inside corner doesn't count toward the minimum. If the countertops for two work centers are contiguous, the length of the combined countertop should be the longer of the two, plus 12 inches.

Primary Work Centers

The primary centers are those that must be included in every kitchen. These should be the first functional areas designated in the new design.

Cleanup Center

Although your kitchen may feature more than one sink, the primary sink is the heart of the cleanup center, which also includes the dishwasher, drain area, disposer, and trash and recycling bins. At least two waste receptacles are recommended. There should be at least 24 inches of counter space on one side of the sink, and 18 inches on the other. Allow 3 inches between the edge of the sink and the inside corner of a countertop. Determine by your dishwashing style whether the dishwasher should be on the right or the left of the sink. There should be 21 inches of standing space on both sides of its open door, and no more than 36 inches from the edge of the dishwasher to the edge of the sink. All electrical receptacles within 6 feet of a sink must be GFCI protected. The kitchen should have two waste receptacles.

Cooking Center

Depending on your cooking style, different appliances will be appropriate for your cooking center, but it should include as fundamentals a surface cooking appliance—either the range top or a separate cooktop—and an oven, and possibly a microwave. There should be at least 15 inches of counter space on one side of the cooktop, and at least 9 inches on the other. If the cooktop is next to an end wall, it must have 3 inches of clearance; the wall must have a flame-retardant surface of ceramic, stone, or stainless steel; and there should be 15 inches of counter space on the other side of the cooktop. The cooktop should not be placed beneath an openable window unless there are 3 inches of clearance behind it and 24 inches above it. There should be at least 24 inches of clearance above the cooktop; 30 inches if the overhang is combustible. The cooktop should have a ventilating system, exhausted to the outside, with a minimum air-movement rating of 150 CFM (cubic feet per minute). A fire extinguisher should be located across from the cooktop, and a smoke detector just outside the kitchen.

Refrigerator Center

Most fresh foods are stored in the refrigerator, and it is the first stop for both a shopper with grocery bags, and a cook. There should be at least 15 inches of counter space on the latch side of the refrigerator (or on the left, for a side-by-side); or, the counter may be across from the refrigerator, if no more than 48 inches away. The refrigerator may be located next to an oven if each is properly insulated. A separate freezer needn't be located in the refrigerator center.

Food-Preparation Center

An area between the cleanup center and the refrigerator center is ideally situated for the food-preparation center. This counter may be used for other activities when meals are not being prepared. The recommended locations are next to a sink, between a sink and cooktop, or between a sink and refrigerator. For kitchens designed for only one cook, there should be at least 36 inches of uninterrupted counter space. For multiple cooks, each needs 36 inches of space. Two cooks working side by side should have 72 inches of straight, continuous counter space. A major appliance, such as a dishwasher, should not be located within the food-preparation center. However, a garbage can or compost bin for food waste should be included.

Secondary Work Centers

The number and type of secondary work centers depend on the additional activities you perform in your kitchen. Secondary work centers often include a specialty cooking area—such as for a wok or for baking—or a bar sink.

Secondary Sink

Recommended by the NKBA, a secondary sink is useful for food preparation and entertaining and is often incorporated into a bar. It may be smaller than the primary sink, but it should have hot and cold water and a garbage disposer. If part of a bar, there should be storage space for washing supplies and for glasses and mixers. A small refrigerator and ice maker are also handy for a bar. If you have a large family or entertain a lot, an additional dishwasher can also be incorporated. A secondary sink may be located 3 inches from an inside corner of the counter, so long as there are at least 21 inches of counter space after turning the corner; if not, the sink should be at least 18 inches from the corner.

Plan landing space within the refrigerator center to set groceries while putting them away. The ideal landing is a minimum of 15 inches wide on the latch side of the refrigerator; it can also be located across from the appliance. The landing for this subzero refrigerator doubles as a food-preparation surface next to the cooktop.

Ovens

Some cooks prefer the oven to be separate from the cooktop. Ovens may be positioned under the counter or in a wall-oven cabinet. Each oven should have 15 inches of counter space next to or above it. This counter may also be across from the oven if the distance is no more than 48 inches and if the passageway is not a primary traffic area. Ovens may be located next to the refrigerator if both are properly insulated.

A relatively smaller and freestanding appliance, the microwave oven may have its own center, be incorporated into the cooktop or oven center, or be located in the refrigerator center. The microwave calls for 15 inches of counter space above, beside, or below it. The bottom edge of the microwave should fall between the counter and the user's shoulder; the most convenient height is at the user's elbow, plus or minus 6 inches.

Eating Area

Opting for an in-room eating space depends on the size of the kitchen and your family's

In kitchen design, the eating and communications areas are considered secondary work centers. Here, the two centers are combined in a light-filled space on the short leg of an L-shaped room. The eating area is served by the handy island cleanup center: a second sink in the island, a dishwasher behind the magazine rack (see page 91), a dish-drain cupboard for everyday dishes across from it, and flatware and linen storage in the baskets under the desk. The pantry wall of this kitchen is pictured on page 52.

An in-kitchen desk provides a space to grab some computer time while dinner cooks. A communications center used exclusively for work allows you to leave projects in progress without fear of them being disturbed by other kitchen activities. However, because the desk countertop here matches others in the room, it can be cleared and used as a serving buffet when the family entertains.

life-style. Minimum counter or table space for each person is 24 inches wide by 12 inches deep. Chair or stool space should measure 24 to 30 inches square; chair space plus a walkway should measure 36 to 42 inches. Heights of eating surfaces vary: Counter height is 36 inches from the floor; table height, 30 inches; bar height, 42 to 44 inches. Chairs and stools must be proportioned accordingly.

Communications Center

One of the most significant aspects of the modern kitchen is the need for a dedicated office area. Ideally, a home office has a horizontal work space that is not used for other purposes, so that work may be left out during food preparation and eating. Plan storage and file drawers, telephone receptacle, and surge-protected electrical receptacles for office machines. Also consider various media requirements for intercom, TV, cable, and speakers.

Work Triangles

The traditional kitchen work triangle was formed by drawing lines to connect the three primary appliances: range, sink, and refrigerator. Although every kitchen must have at least one primary work triangle, the wealth of work centers in the modern kitchen cannot be forced into one triangle. While the work-triangle concept is still relevant today, it has been expanded to include two or more interacting triangles. Triangles incorporating secondary work centers can be designed to suit your specific needs. For example, a secondary triangle can be formed by combining the refrigerator/microwave/eating space or the refrigerator/baking center/wall oven.

Defined as the shortest walking distance connecting three work centers, the perimeter of each triangle should measure 12 to 26 feet. A two-cook kitchen should have two primary triangles, each with a sink, refrigerator, and cooking appliance. But this doesn't mean you must double up on everything. The triangles may share a point, or even a leg, so long as the legs don't cross. The best point to share is the refrigerator. Then, for example, one cook can use the primary sink and the cooktop, the other cook uses the secondary sink and the wall oven, and both use the refrigerator—without crossing paths. If the triangles have a common leg, the two cooks can share the refrigerator and the sink, while one uses the cooktop and the other uses the microwave.

An island, peninsula, or table should not jut more than 12 inches into a work triangle, nor should a door swing open into one. No two primary work centers may be separated by a tall cabinet, refrigerator, or wall.

Traffic Patterns

The new NKBA–Minnesota guidelines regarding kitchen-traffic corridors differentiate between working aisles and passageways, and call for different dimensions for each.

A working aisle has a work center on one or both sides. A passageway is a thoroughfare with a work center on one side or none at all. A working aisle should be at least 42 inches wide; 48 inches wide for two cooks. A passageway with no work centers should measure at least 36 inches wide; corner-to-corner clearance between cabinets should be a minimum of 32 inches. A door into the kitchen should have a minimum clearance of 32 inches, wider for wheelchair access.

Traffic should never be routed through a working aisle or a primary work triangle. Traffic through a secondary work triangle should be avoided, although sometimes this is not possible.

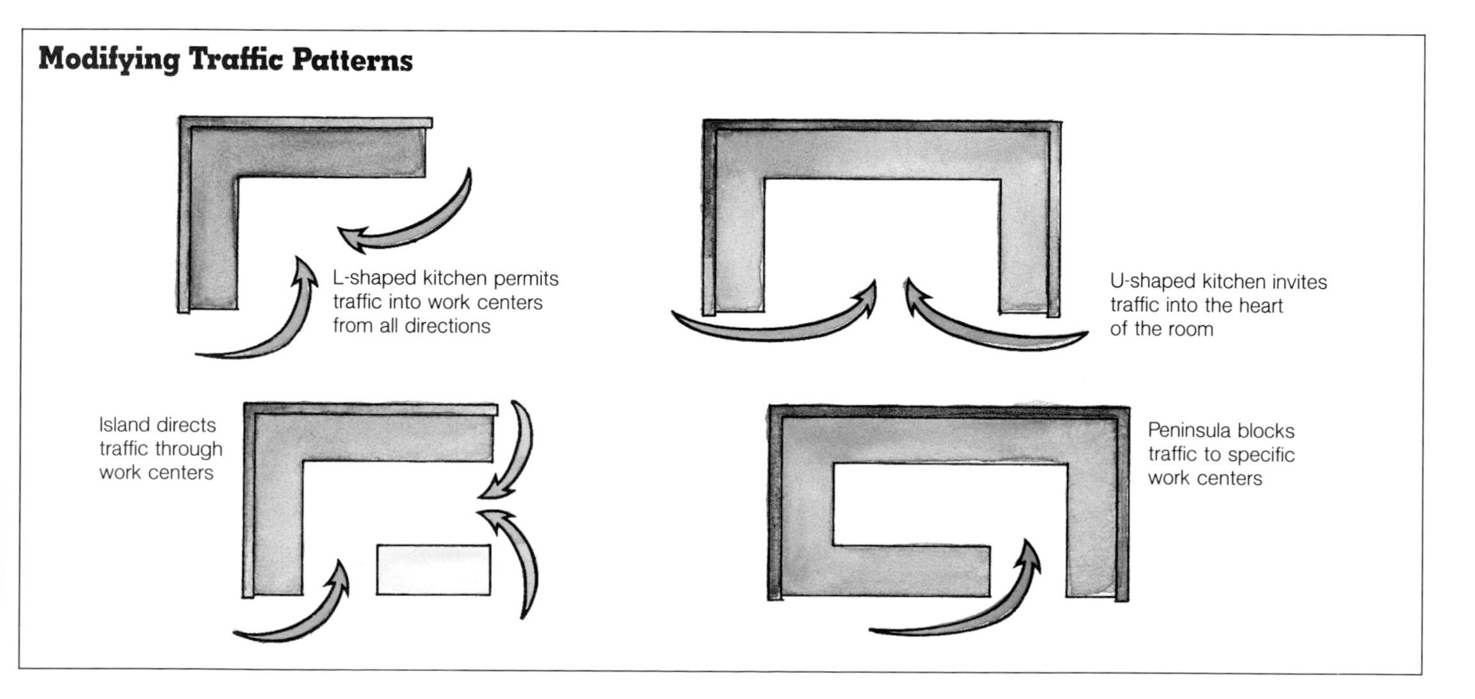

Modifying Traffic Patterns

DRAWING PLANS

A plan is a graphic representation, drawn to scale, showing the exact size and location of every feature in a room. Use plans to visualize the kitchen layout, determine the exact size of fixtures and appliances, route utilities, and obtain building permits.

The Base Plan

Once you've collected all your ideas and formulated some preferences, you're ready to jump into designing the space. Start by drawing an accurate plan of the existing kitchen, in ½-inch scale.

Measuring the Space

To draw a plan of the existing kitchen, you must first take precise measurements, which you will then scale down and transfer to paper. Start by sketching on a large pad of paper the basic outlines of the kitchen. Include doors, windows, trim, half walls, duct chases, pantry, and any other architectural features. Use this sketch to record your measurements.

The best tool for measuring is an 8-foot carpenter's folding rule with a slide-out extension for fractions of inches. An adequate substitute is a 25- or 30-foot retractable steel tape measure. Have a companion help you hold the tool. Use inches only, rather than feet and inches, for all measurements. This will make the transfer to a ½-inch scale easier to calculate.

To measure, start in one corner of the room, at about waist height. Extend the rule along the wall to the next feature—for example, the outside edge of the window trim—and write this measurement at the corresponding location on the sketch, in inches, to the nearest ⅛ inch. Next, measure across the window to the opposite outside trim edge, and note the window measurement. Continue measuring the wall, noting each feature separately, until you reach the next corner. Now, measure the entire wall, corner to corner. Add together your first measurements; the result should equal the second measurement exactly. If not, take all the measurements again, until they match.

Measure and record each wall this way, around the perimeter of the kitchen. There can be no fudging! If opposite walls that should be the same width are off by an inch or so, do not be alarmed—not all rooms are square. Note the differences.

To check whether a corner is square, make a mark exactly 3 feet out from the corner on one wall, and a mark 4 feet out on the other wall. Measure the diagonal distance between the two marks; it should be exactly 5 feet. If it's more than 5 feet, the corner angle is greater than 90 degrees; if it's less than 5 feet, the corner angle is smaller than 90 degrees. Note this on your sketch.

Next, measure the positions of electrical switches and receptacles, water pipes, vents, telephone jacks, the gas line, and other utilities and record them on your sketch (both distance from the corner and height off the floor).

On the sink wall, measure from one corner to the center of the sink. Measure the height of windows and their distance from the floor, the height and width of door and window trim, and the positions of stairways.

Measure built-in shelves, pass-throughs—every architectural detail. Measure and note the thickness of each wall (minus any trim). If you cannot see the wall profile, insert a thin wire through the wall and measure the difference. Also measure and record the height of the ceiling.

If you are considering expanding the kitchen into any adjoining rooms, add them to your sketch, and measure them the same way you did the kitchen, including the thickness of the walls between them. All of these measurements will be used to construct an accurate base plan of the existing kitchen.

Putting the Plan on Paper

Begin the plan by taping a piece of graph paper to a drawing board. In one corner, write ½":1' to indicate the scale used (½ inch equals 1 foot). This scale should appear on all drawings. Divide the inch measurements on your sketch by 12 (to get the number of feet). Then convert each foot to a half inch and each fraction of a foot to its corresponding fraction of a half inch. This gives you the measurements for the scale drawing. An architect's scale simplifies the conversion process immensely.

Using a straightedge, draw light lines representing the basic perimeter of the kitchen, using the converted measurements. Use the lines on the graph paper as a guide. Around the outside of this perimeter, draw lines representing the wall thicknesses. Then add the perimeters of any other rooms or spaces you measured.

Now, go back and put in the details. Working your way around the plan perimeter, draw each wall segment, window, door, trim piece, duct chase, pass-through, and every other permanent feature, based on the measurements you took. Indicate the exact positions of the receptacles, switches, pipes, vents, and other utilities. Indicate whether doors swing in or out, left or right. As you draw each feature, note its actual measurements on the plan.

Make several high-quality photocopies of your final base plan to keep as spares and for sketching ideas. Never use photocopies of photocopies for scaled design work. The slight distortions caused by most copy machines will be accentuated and can throw off your measurements.

Use a copy of the base plan to draw an existing plan—one showing all features in the existing kitchen. Again, use exact measurements. Draw the kitchen as it is now, complete with cabinets, counters, appliances, light fixtures, and furniture. If the kitchen is fairly standard, a kitchen-fixture template will have cutouts of the

The Base Plan

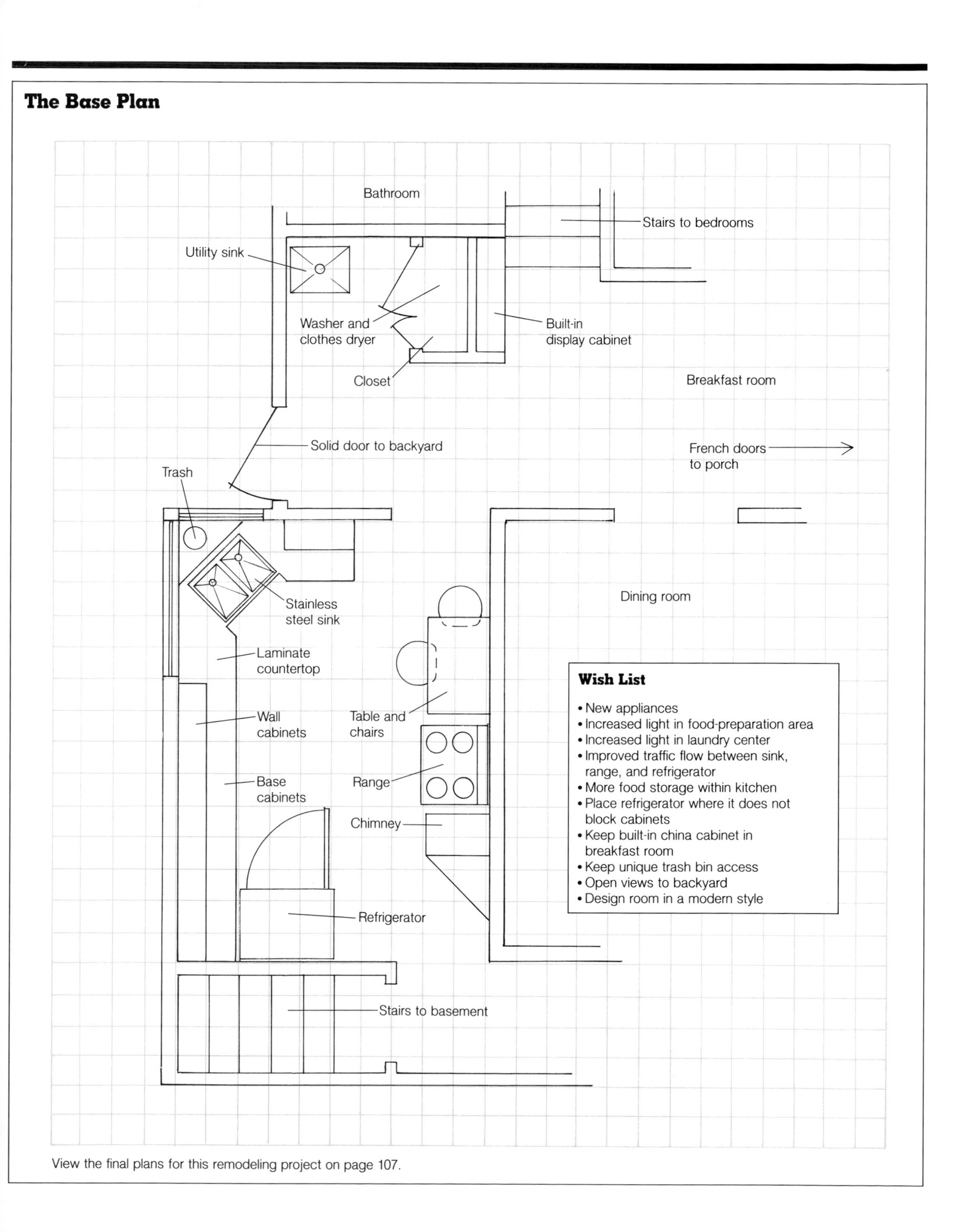

Wish List

- New appliances
- Increased light in food-preparation area
- Increased light in laundry center
- Improved traffic flow between sink, range, and refrigerator
- More food storage within kitchen
- Place refrigerator where it does not block cabinets
- Keep built-in china cabinet in breakfast room
- Keep unique trash bin access
- Open views to backyard
- Design room in a modern style

View the final plans for this remodeling project on page 107.

right dimensions that you can trace. You now have a bird's-eye view of the faults and virtues of the existing kitchen. Save copies of this existing plan; it may be required by the building department.

Making Bubble Drawings

Next, it's time to use your imagination. Tape tracing paper over the original base plan (or use the photocopies) and sketch circles showing where you'd like your various activities to take place. Consult your wish list of desired activities and, using the information from the NKBA–Minnesota study, locate the primary and secondary work centers.

Bubble drawings provide a graphic representation of the activity areas in a room and the flow of traffic through it; they show which arrangements work and which don't. Professionals call this a motion study. For those of you frustrated by precise drafting techniques, this is the fun part.

If you've always wanted an eat-in kitchen, circle an area designated as the eating center and try to build around it. Be creative. Close off doorways, eliminate walls; it's just on paper at this point.

When a bubble plan looks as though it's coming together, use the template to start adding appliances, cabinets, and other fixtures to see what fits. Use a different-colored pencil to test traffic patterns.

When you're satisfied with one plan, draw a new one! Move the appliances, move the doorways, and see what happens to the work triangles and the traffic flow. You'll use lots

Bubble Drawings

Version 1

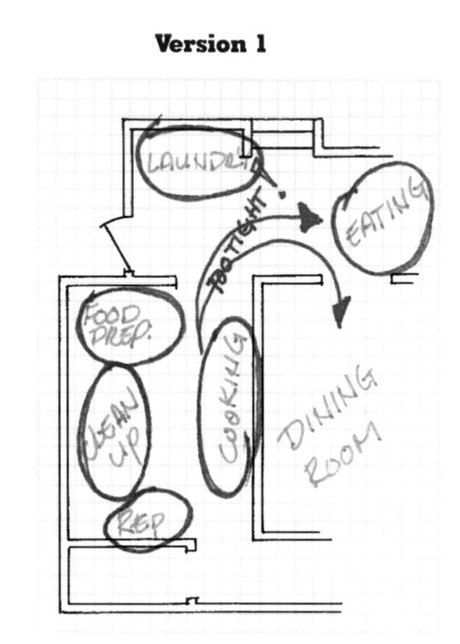

Drawback: does not allow for minimum space requirements

Version 2

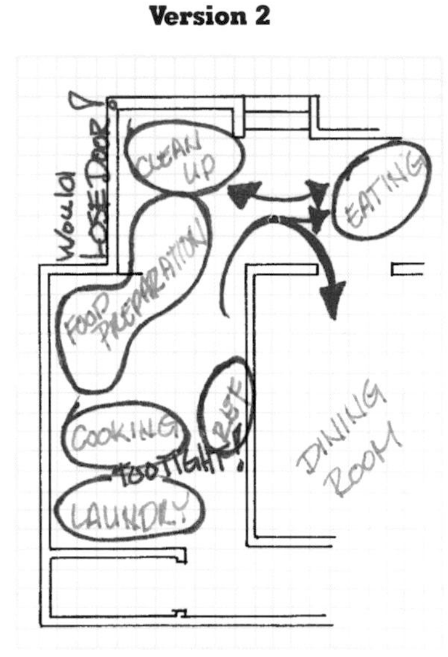

Drawbacks: destroys access to and natural light from backyard

Version 3

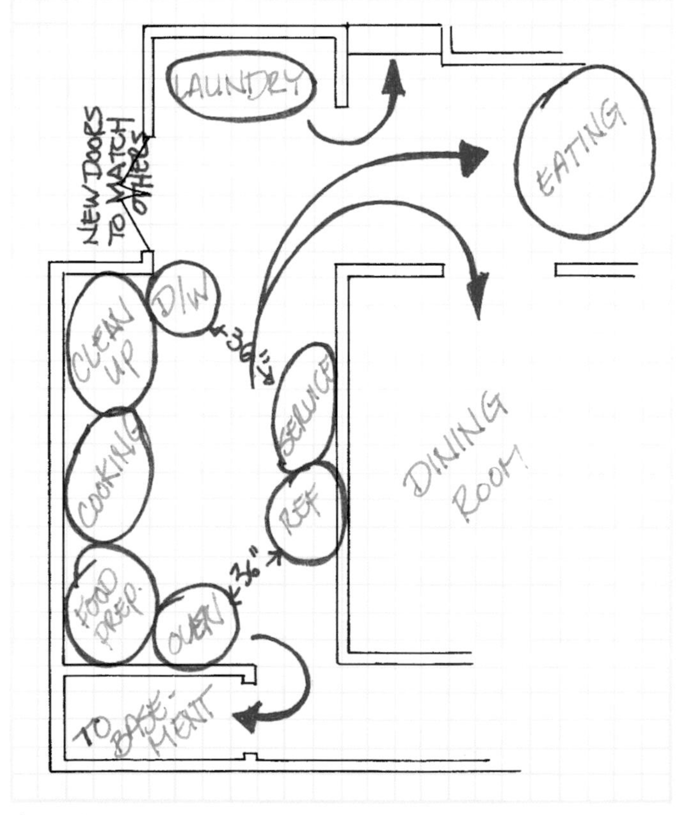

A sensible basis for a preliminary floor plan: fulfills most items on wish list while disturbing the fewest plumbing fixtures

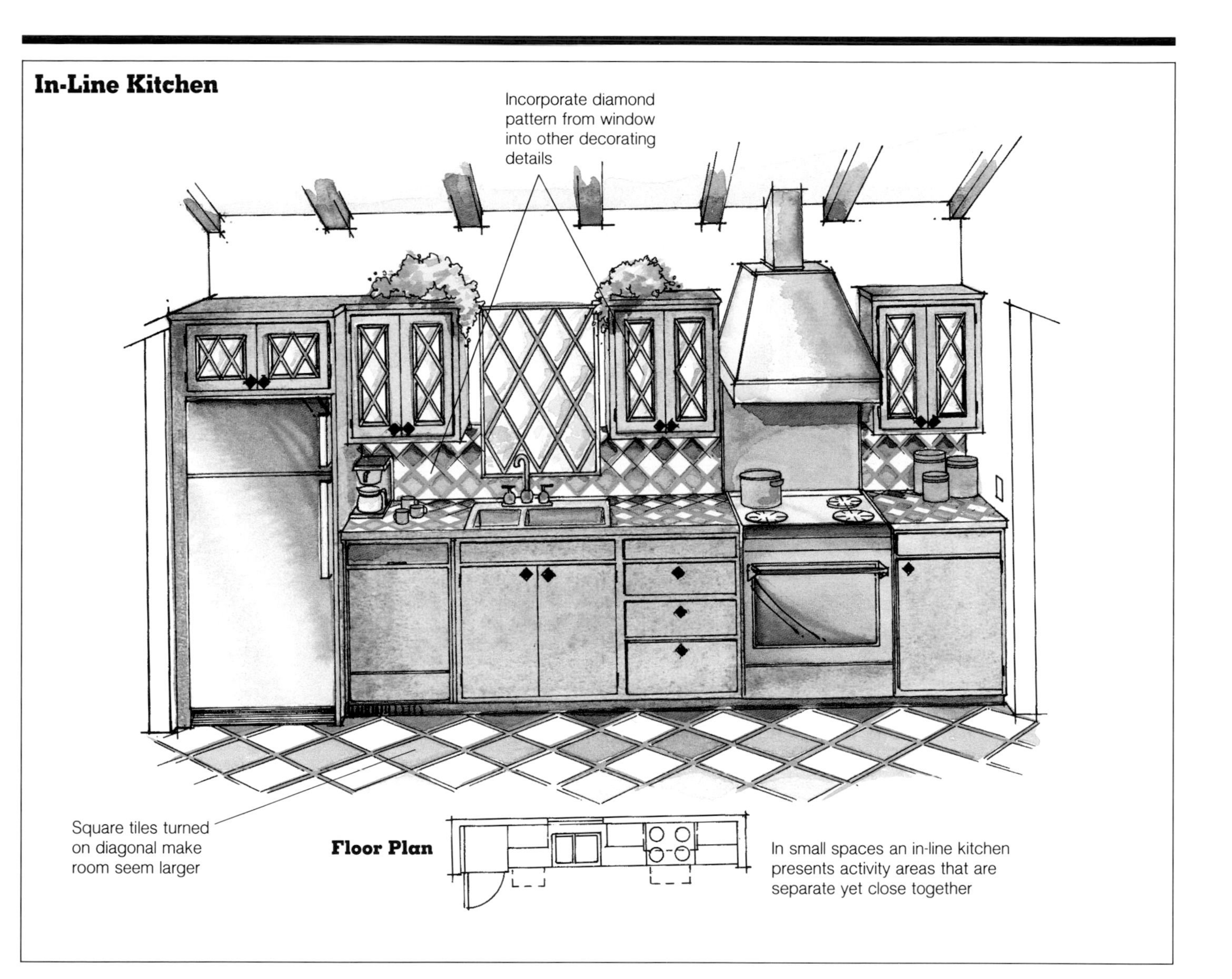

of paper; this is idea time. For this exercise, you may wish to make templates by tracing the kitchen fixtures onto index cards and cutting them out, so you can move them around like pieces on a gameboard.

Evaluate each bubble plan, comparing it with the existing kitchen and with your wish list. Does it fulfill your family's activity needs and wants? Does it solve space and traffic-flow problems?

Investigate various kitchen shapes and configurations. Would adding a peninsula or island fulfill counter space and work center requirements?

Draw lines that show the movement among work centers during typical kitchen activities. Are they too close or too far away? Will two cooks run into each other?

Next, draw lines indicating traffic through the kitchen, in and out of every door. Does this traffic flow cut through a work triangle? Is it awkward to get from one part of the room to another?

Draw lines of sight showing views out the kitchen windows and views of the kitchen from other rooms.

Don't be concerned with materials and styles at this point, but do start thinking about your budget. If the plan calls for major structural or utility changes, such as building an addition or rerouting the plumbing system, can you afford it? A creative design can still achieve a desired feel and flavor, even with a limited budget.

Discuss the bubble drawings with family and friends—great insight can come from a fresh perspective. If you can, put the plans aside for a few weeks to distance yourself from your work, and then reexamine the plans to see if your perspective—and ideals—have changed over time.

Understanding Shapes

The confines of the room you are remodeling or adding will be rectangular or square, but the way the doors, windows, countertops, and other features are placed defines its shape. No one shape is better or worse than any other—just different. Play with various shape options as you develop your bubble drawings. Understanding the common shapes defined here will give you a reference for when you discuss the design with remodeling professionals.

If space allows, building peninsulas and islands within the kitchen adds work centers and storage space without adding square footage to the room. The shape of these features should complement the shape of the room.

In-Line

Placing all the work centers in a straight line works well for small kitchens and for kitchen areas in studios that will be closed off with sliding or folding doors or a screen (see page 35). However, an in-line plan can also work successfully in a large, long kitchen, so long as you allow for plenty of space between work centers.

Galley

Like its namesake on a ship, a galley kitchen places the work centers in two parallel lines with an aisle between. This layout works best when one end of the kitchen is a wall and the other end opens onto an eating area, family room or to the outside. The aisle needs to be at least 36 inches wide; 48 inches is better.

Galley Kitchen

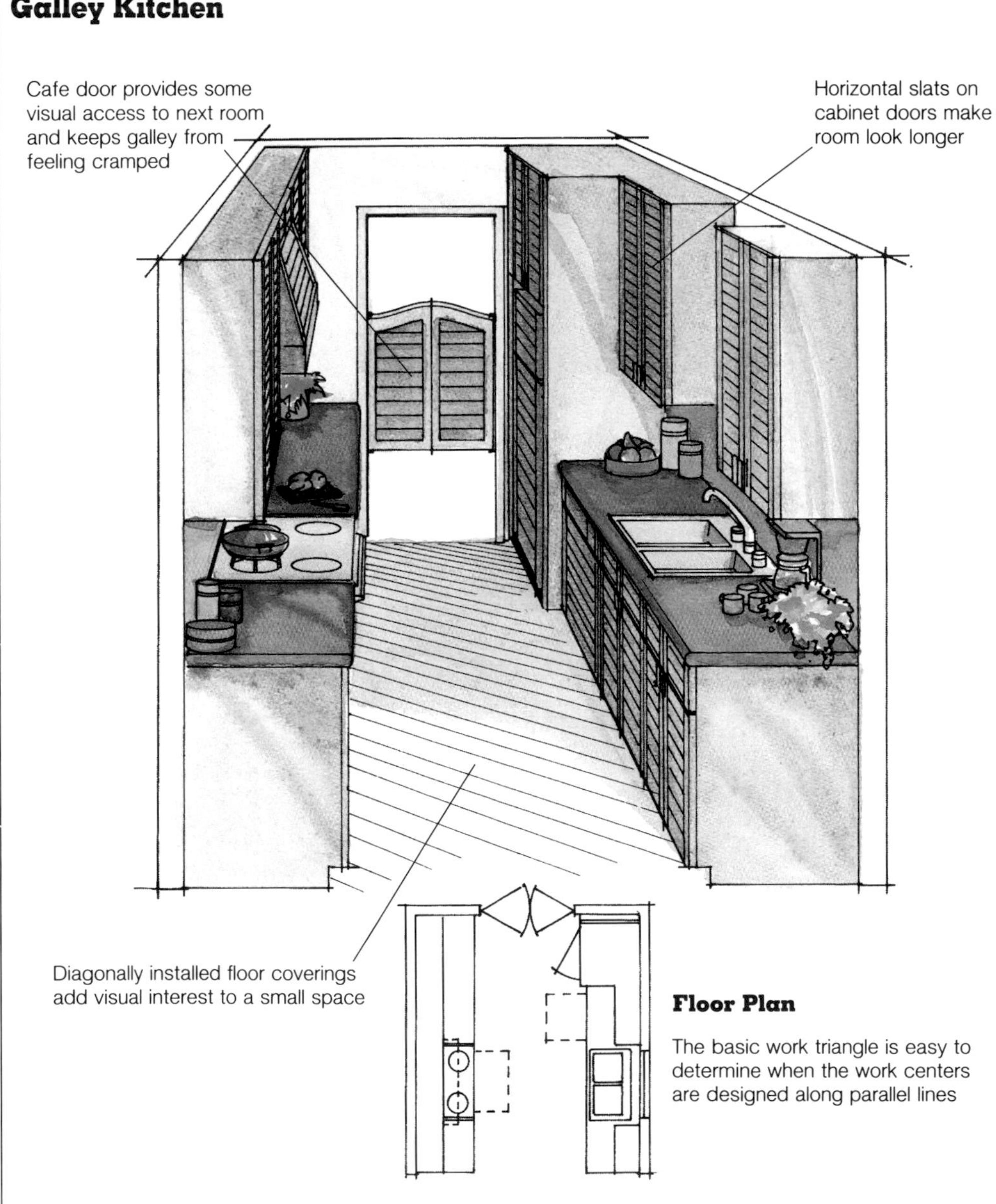

Floor Plan

The basic work triangle is easy to determine when the work centers are designed along parallel lines

L-Shaped

Named for the letter it resembles, the L-shaped kitchen is formed by two legs of equal or unequal lengths joined at a right angle (see opposite page). To avoid diminishing the apparent size of the kitchen, tall appliances and cabinets should be placed at the end of one leg rather than at the ends of both.

Using a peninsula, form an L-shaped kitchen within a larger rectangular room to divide the space into separate food-preparation and eating centers. This is a popular solution if you'd like a discrete eating area and do not have a dining room.

U-Shaped

Placing work centers along three sides of a square space creates a U-shaped kitchen (see page 38). Often the sink is the focal point of the base of the U, with the cooking center on one side and the refrigerator center on the other. One leg may be a peninsula rather than a full wall. If the U is wide enough, consider an island in the center. Minimum U-shaped kitchen width is 12 feet for an island 2 feet wide.

Variations

The basic kitchen shapes can be adjusted to your room and activity needs. The basic L and U shapes can be bisected by a door or passageway. The U

L-Shaped Kitchen

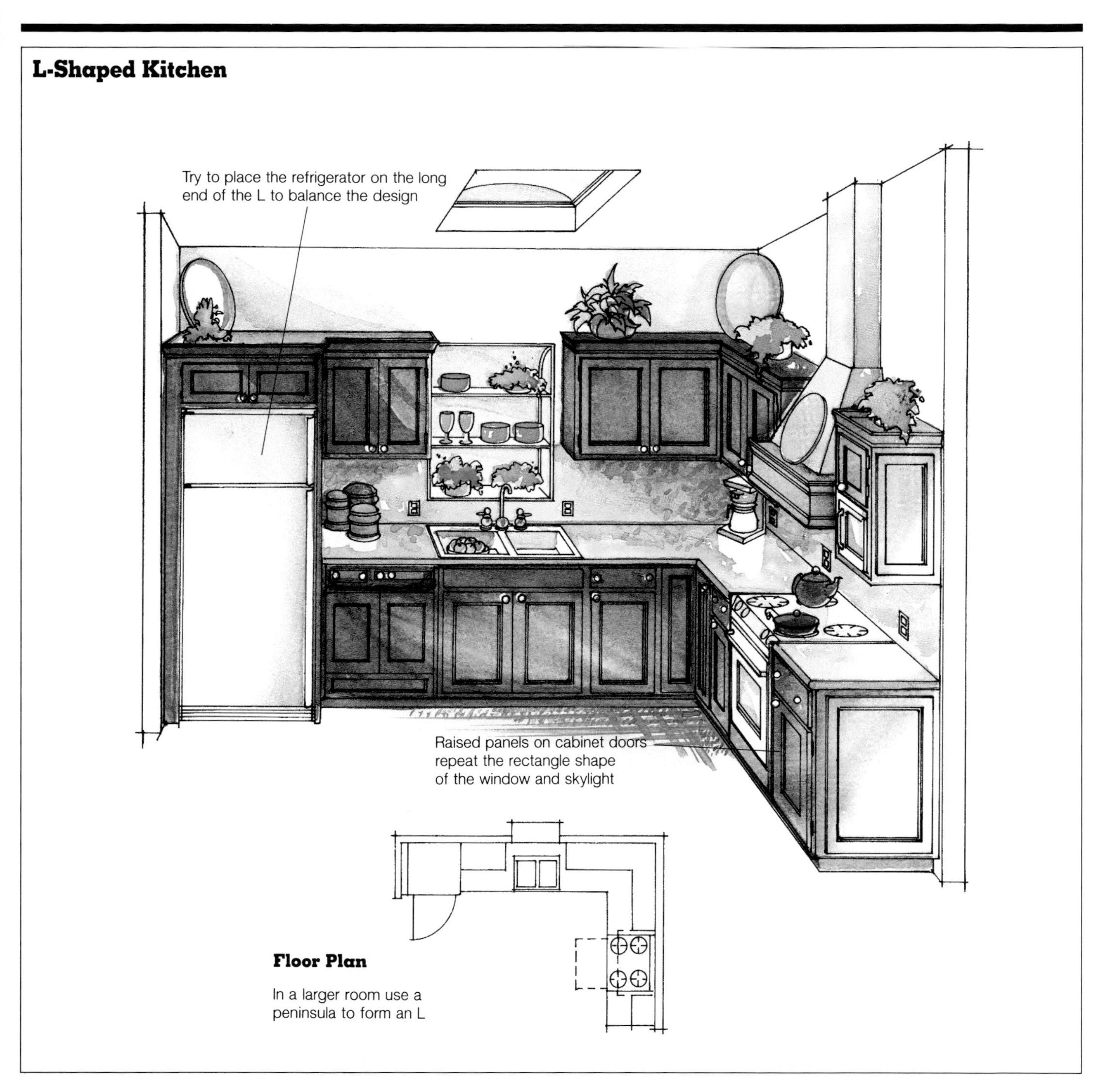

shape can be augmented with a short fourth wall or peninsula. Adding a short peninsula within the basic square kitchen turns it into a G-shaped room. Setting any of the basic shapes on an angle or a curve may fit your space allotment better and may solve any traffic-pattern problems.

Peninsulas

A partition connected to one wall and dividing the space within the kitchen is called a peninsula. It can be created as a new design element or by removing a portion of a wall between the kitchen and an adjoining space. Peninsulas are a popular means of adding counter space for various work centers. Install a cooktop and oven in a peninsula, place a hood above it, and it serves as a cooking center. Put in a sink and dishwasher onto base cabinets, and the peninsula becomes the cleanup center.

A cantilever-counter peninsula can serve as an eating or other work center either at the same height as other kitchen counters, stepped up six or eight inches as a bar that screens the kitchen activities from view, or stepped down six or eight inches to table height. Its end can be square, angled, or curved, depending on the design line used within your kitchen.

You can install cabinets, shelves, or other features above a peninsula. Wall cabinets hung from the ceiling above a peninsula will be shorter than standard, ending about eye level. They can be accessed from the kitchen side, the back side, or both. Consider open shelves or glass doors to maintain as much light as possible between spaces.

Islands

A freestanding unit within a kitchen, either portable or installed, is called an island. Design the size of the island in balance with the scale of the room. The bigger your kitchen

U-Shaped Kitchen

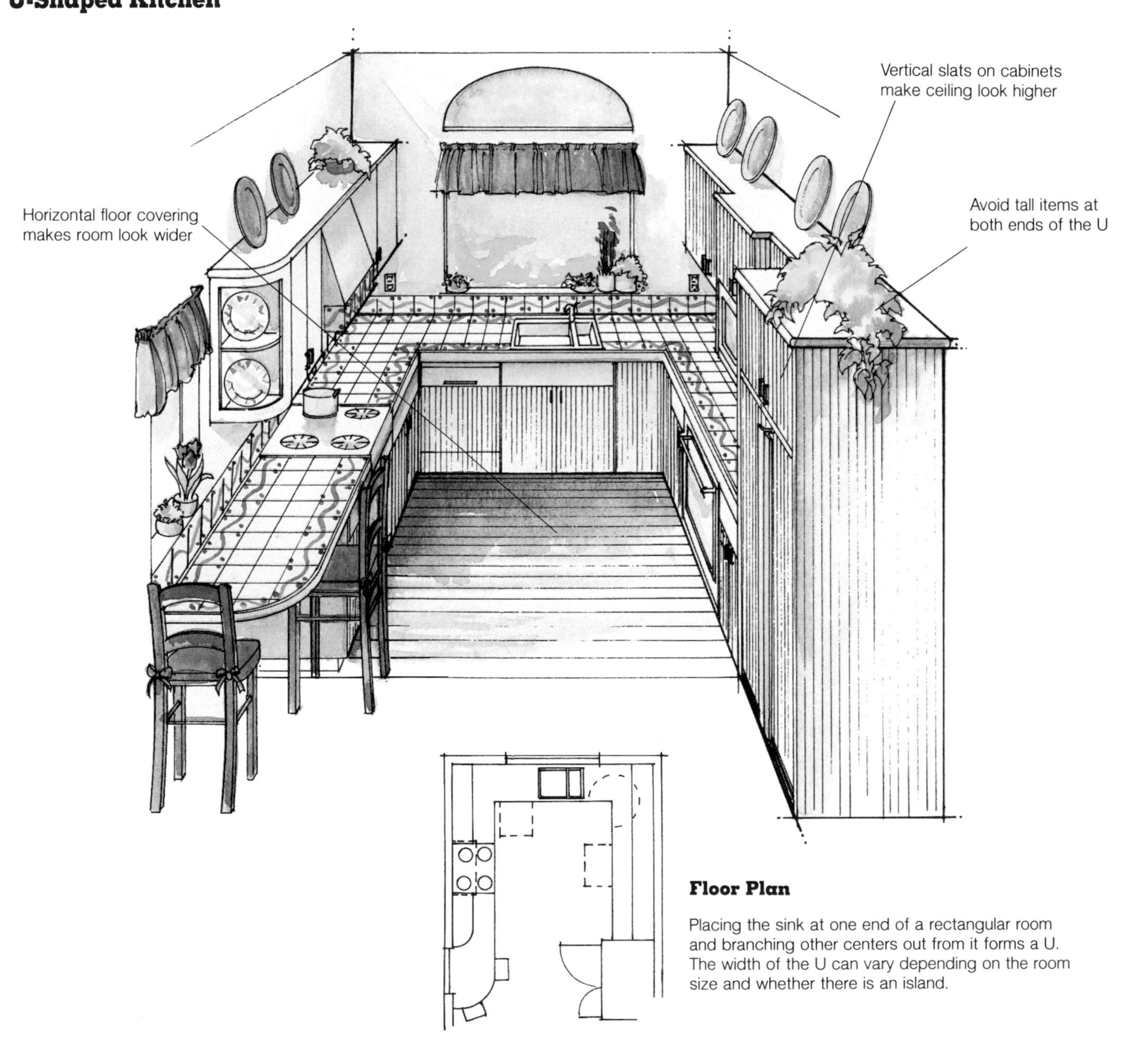

Floor Plan

Placing the sink at one end of a rectangular room and branching other centers out from it forms a U. The width of the U can vary depending on the room size and whether there is an island.

is, the larger the island can be. The minimum size for an island is 2 feet by 3 feet. Allow for a 3-foot-wide aisle on all sides of an island.

Build an island from base cabinets, add a countertop, and use it as a leg for several different work triangles. Islands make excellent secondary work centers and are especially useful as food-preparation areas. For example, the cabinets can be designed to hold specialty cooking items, such as those needed for baking. If the island primarily supports a baking center, you may want to top it with a stone slab; if used mainly for cutting and chopping, consider butcher block. Topping an island with a different material than that used for the other countertops adds texture and visual interest to the room. Islands can be stepped up or down in height depending on their uses.

Square Kitchen

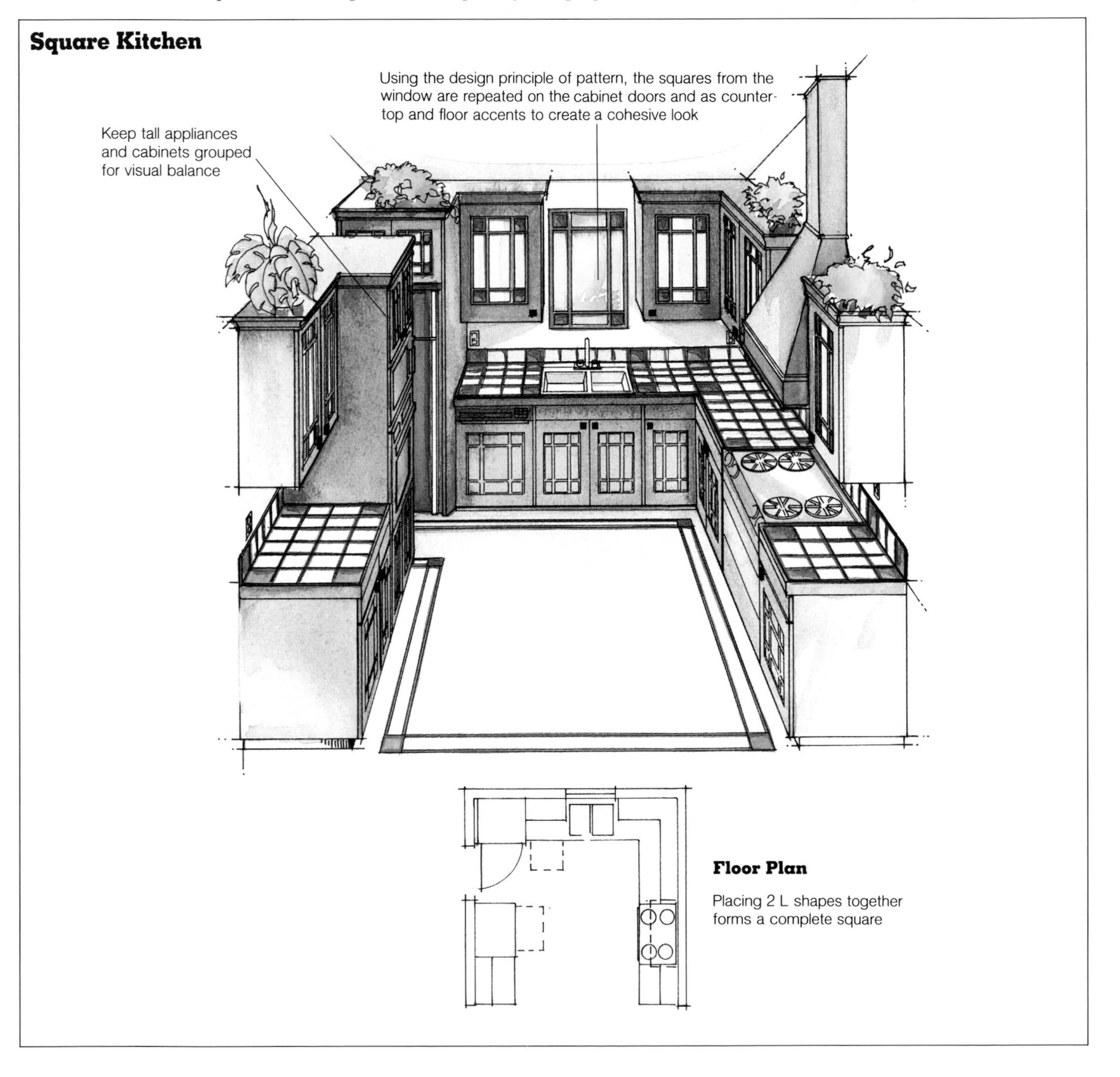

Curvilinear Kitchen

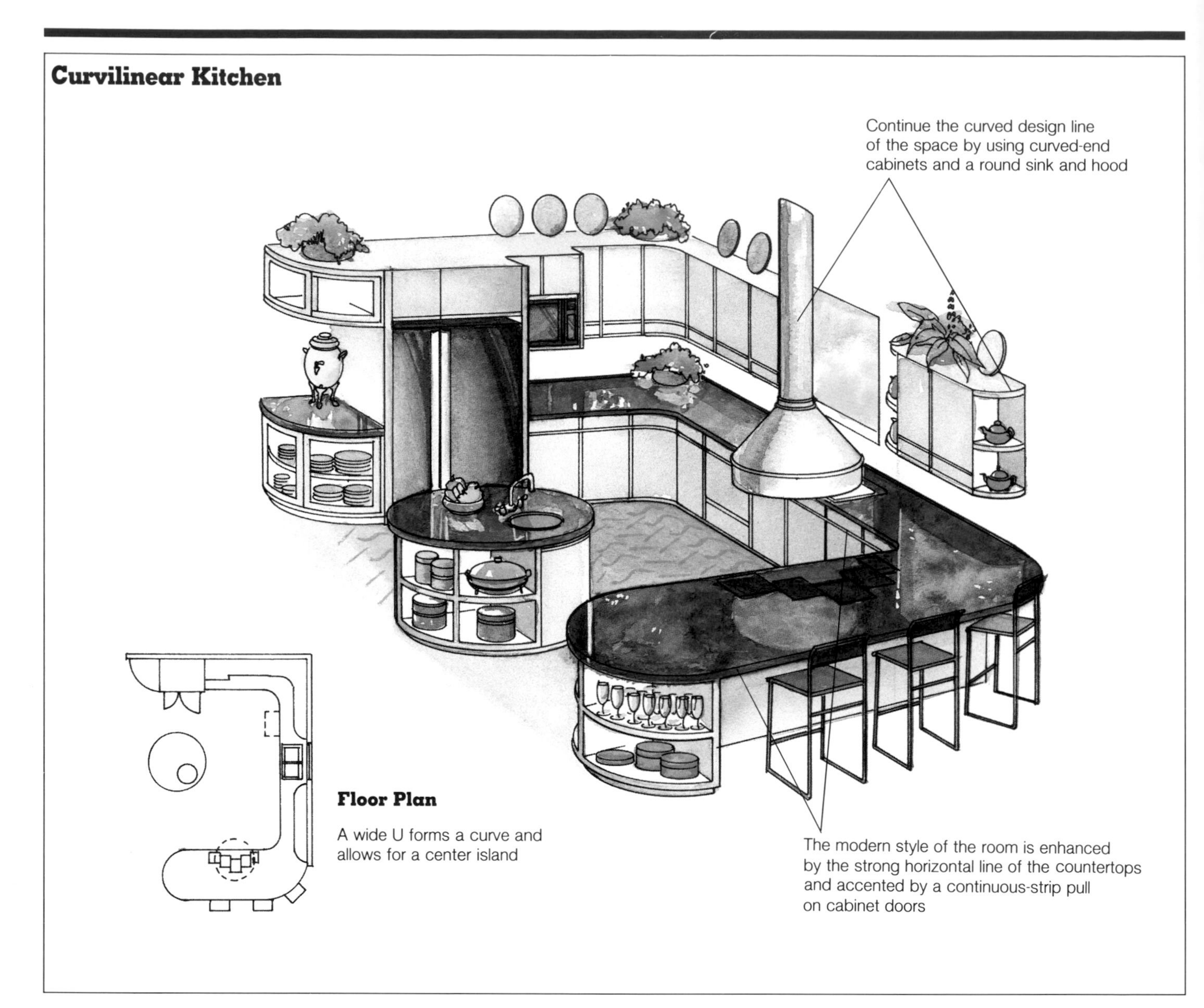

Floor Plan

A wide U forms a curve and allows for a center island

Islands can be plumbed, wired, and used as primary work centers as well. Include a cooktop and oven and use the island as the cooking center; install a sink and dishwasher and make it the primary clean-up center; or put in an under-counter refrigerator and a small sink and the island becomes a bar for entertaining.

Consider the shape and design lines of the room when determining the island shape. Match a rectangular island to the rectangular lines of the room, a square island to a square room. Create a triangle within an L-shaped room by customizing cabinet units, thus setting up a diagonal design scheme. Use curved-end cabinets to harmonize with other curved elements within the room.

Developing a Preliminary Plan

One bubble drawing will eventually emerge as the most elegant and practical solution to your needs. With a copy of the base plan as your guide, use your ½-inch scale or template to lay out the basic elements of your new kitchen.

The preliminary plan is a guide for choosing finishes, fixtures, and appliances; make it as complete and detailed as possible. Cast a critical eye on the minute details. Check the views and traffic patterns.

The plans must remain preliminary until you know exactly which construction elements, cabinets, fixtures, and appliances will be installed. Choosing them wisely is the subject of the next two chapters. Make the final plan only after reading these.

Creating Islands

Minimum Dimensions

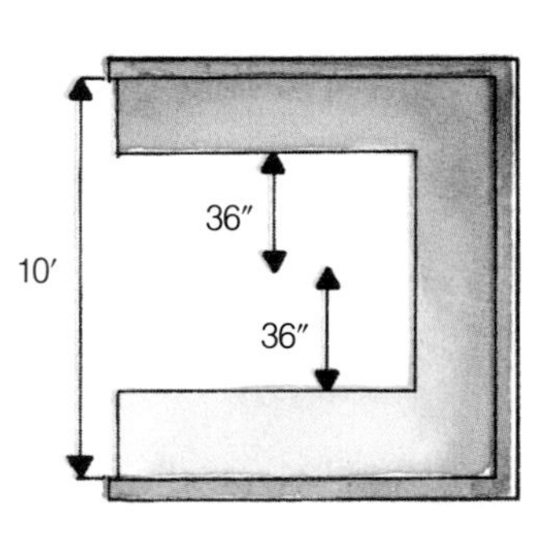

Minimum 36″ aisle requirements do not allow for an island

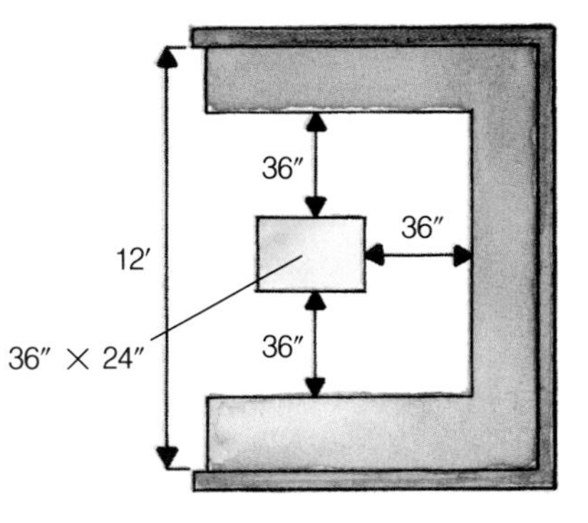

Minimum island size and aisle width

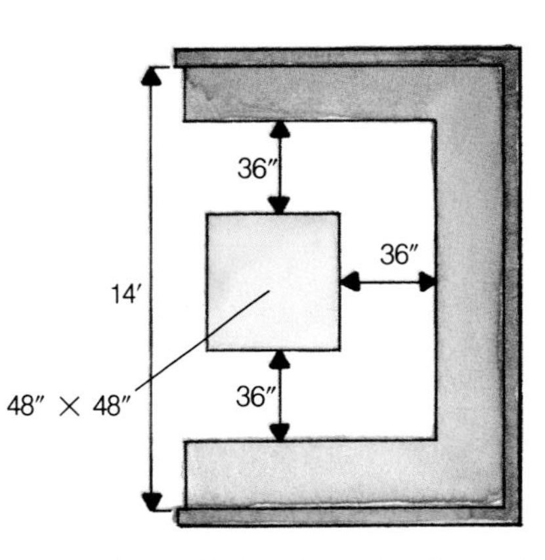

A large kitchen allows for a larger island

Cooktop

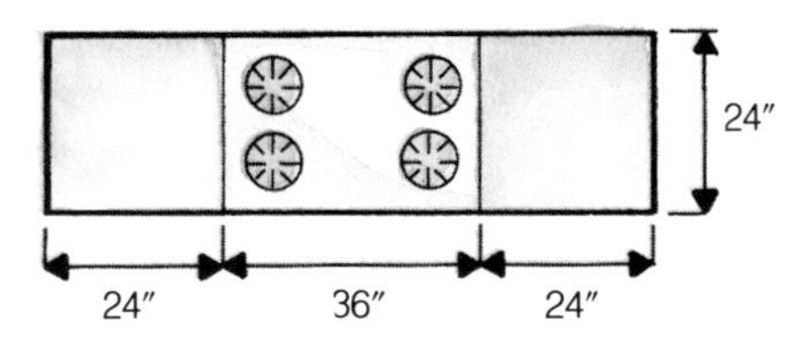

Cleanup

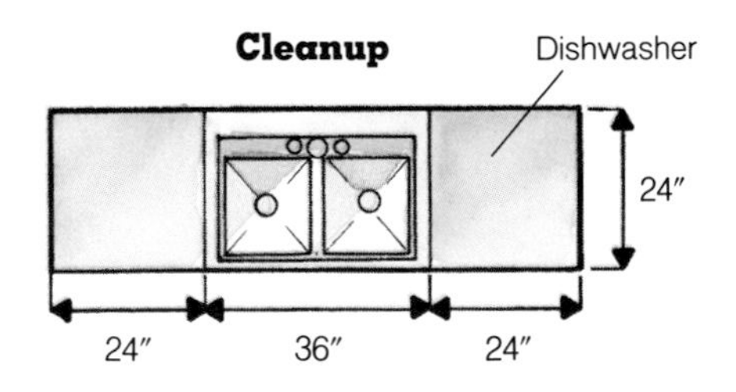

Eating

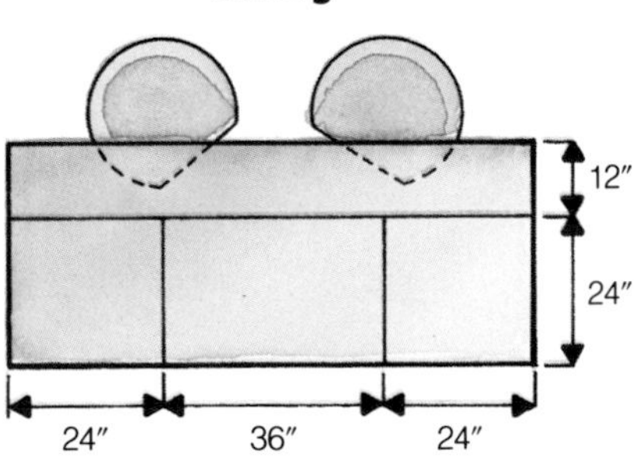

Base Configurations

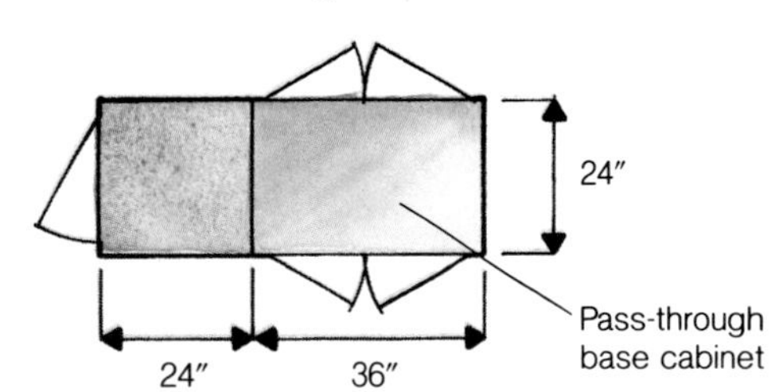

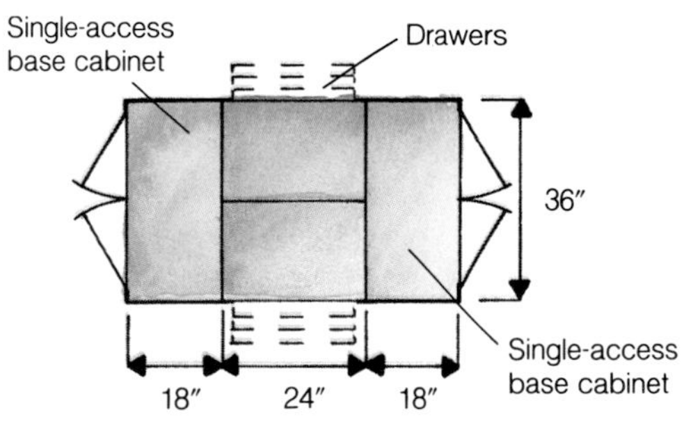

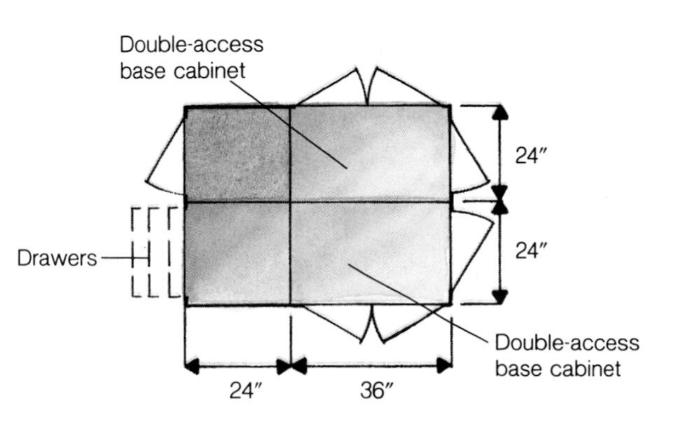

SPECIFYING THE CONSTRUCTION ELEMENTS

Conceiving the kitchen of your dreams takes imagination and flair. Turning those dreams into reality requires close attention to the nuts-and-bolts details of kitchen construction. The structure of the walls, floor, and ceiling; the systems and utilities hidden within them; and the finishes that cover their surfaces determine more than anything else whether the kitchen meets your needs as a pleasant and practical place to work and entertain. The variety of finish materials available for the modern kitchen allows you to develop the design you want in a number of price ranges.

Some construction elements can be personal as well as practical. Specialty tiles in this backsplash reflect one homeowner's dual career: She is both a musician and a cookbook author. The cabinets reflect the talents of the co-owner: They were designed and built by his construction company.

ALLS

While deciding which walls stay, which walls go, and where new walls are needed, you must also determine what work must be done within the walls themselves to make them sound. Once their placement is set, all walls must be finished to suit the new look.

Keeping Walls

Leaving an existing wall right where it is saves much effort and expense, but it doesn't mean the wall must remain untouched. Check the condition of the wall surface; if it has more than superficial damage, is not flat, flexes when pressed on, or shows obvious patching, the surface material—usually wallboard or plaster over lath—should be torn off the underlying studs. In a major remodeling job this usually entails removing the entire wall surface, because it is easier to refinish a wall from corner to corner than to patch a large area neatly.

Exposing the framing this way has several other advantages. With the wall surface removed, the wiring, pipes, ducts, and insulation can be inspected, and the framing can be examined for insect damage, rot, and construction errors. Watch for the following common problems:

- Headers that are not adequate for the span they cover
- Studs that have been cut away and not supported
- A sink vent stack that does not extend through the roof
- Hot wires hanging loose in the wall
- A range hood duct that vents into the attic

Alterations to the electrical and plumbing systems are most easily done with the wall wide open. You can even rebuild the wall itself. With the framing exposed, for example, you can convert a typical 2-by-4 stud wall to a 2-by-6 wet wall—thick enough to contain 3- and 4-inch stack pipes—by nailing 2 by 2s to the studs.

If you decide not to expose the framing on a retained wall, you may incur unexpected expenses related to conditions hidden inside. A contractor bidding on a kitchen job often specifies in the bid that corrections to unforeseen problems carry an extra charge.

Adding Interior Walls

If you're lucky enough to have a large space to work with, you may decide to subdivide it into specialized centers—a mud room, a laundry, an office—by adding walls. Such interior walls are also known as partitions.

A partition wall is simple to build and install. The frame, made of 2-by-4 or 2-by-6 studs, is nailed together on the floor and then raised into place. Doorways, pass-throughs, and built-in shelving nooks are framed into the wall at the same time. Once the frame is raised, the planned electrical wiring, plumbing, insulation, duct work, blocking for cabinet supports, and other in-wall systems can be installed efficiently before the frame is enclosed with wallboard.

Partial Walls

Not all walls completely enclose a space. Your kitchen design may include partial walls. A wing wall is a partition that extends only partway across a room. A wing wall is a viable solution for a partially open kitchen design; the wall separates the kitchen from an adjoining room without the feeling of closure that a doorway causes. It can also be used to enclose a refrigerator or end a row of cabinets.

A pony wall, or kneewall, stops below the ceiling, usually at counter height, and provides a casual but definite boundary for peripheral areas of the kitchen, such as the home office desk or the laundry. It can double as a shelf or support a bar counter. A wall with a foot or two of open space above can admit light from another room, thus brightening the kitchen.

Partial walls are built in much the same way as full walls and can support plumbing, electrical wiring, appliances, and cabinets. In fact, cabinets help strengthen such walls. Freestanding walls that do not reach the ceiling must be stabilized by extra supports.

Finish Treatments

Once you've made practical provisions for installing sound walls, you can indulge in the fun of deciding how to decorate them. In the past, poor ventilation and greasy, sooty cooking required that kitchen walls be finished with a wipe-clean surface, but technical advances in ventilation and wall-treatment fabrication have greatly increased the options. The finish treatment you choose must not only be practical but should reflect the look of the kitchen and—especially if the walls are visible from other rooms—the design concept of the entire house. In choosing finish treatments remember that two or three well-coordinated types are often combined in one room.

Paint

Paint offers the most variety for wall color. Many paint dealers now have color-mixing computers that can "look at" a sample of tile, countertop material, or fabric and mix a paint that matches exactly. Paint is an inexpensive and practical choice for a hardworking cook's kitchen, particularly if the walls are within reach of small children. A typical gloss paint is scrubbable and, in case of surface damage, can simply be painted over.

For the kitchen, choose a high-quality wall paint, either latex or oil based, with a gloss or semigloss finish; flat paints are absorbent and difficult to wash.

To estimate the amount of primer and paint needed, multiply the width times the height of each wall or wall segment to get their areas, add them together, then subtract the area of each door and window. Double this figure if applying two coats over a previously painted wall (to cover a dark color with a light one, for example). New kitchens are usually painted before cabinets are installed; retained cabinets do not have to be removed. Remember to add the areas behind appliances. The paint dealer or the label on the paint can will tell you how many square feet each gallon covers.

Wallcoverings

Durable modern wallcoverings can be a smart choice for the kitchen. For large wall expanses in a room you'll inhabit so much, a conservative pattern will feel most comfortable. Used in small areas, however, bold patterns can accent plain painted walls. Patterns that imitate tile or brick are an attractive faux look for a backsplash. Many wallcoverings have matching or coordinating print fabrics for curtains, blinds, or tablecloths. These are detailed in sample books, available from any wallcovering dealer.

For ease of maintenance, choose an all-vinyl or a vinyl-coated wallcovering. Vinyl with a fabric backing is the most durable and is easiest to hang. Make sure the sample book describes the wallcovering as "scrubbable," not just "washable," unless you plan to protect splash areas with sheets of clear acrylic. Avoid delicate papers and textured coverings such as grass cloth or cork.

Wallcoverings cost somewhat more than paint but far less than other specialty finishes, such as wood or tile. Considering its design impact and its durability, wallcovering is an attractive and economical choice.

Wallcoverings are measured by the roll, which, regardless of width, covers about 35 square feet (European wallcoverings will do about 28 square feet). Two or three rolls of wallcovering may come in a single package—check the label. To determine how much you need, measure the area to be covered and add at least 10 percent for waste, trimming, and future patching. Wallcovering tools are specialized but simple and are often available in kits where wallcoverings and adhesives are sold.

In addition to wallcoverings, myriad borders are available, in widths from approximately 2 to 6 inches. They are usually prepasted, and make a strong design accent when used alone or when coordinated with full-wall wallcoverings. In a kitchen, borders can be applied along the ceiling, level with the top edge of wall cabinets and window frames, or at counter level for a chair-rail effect.

Ceramic Tile

Although expensive and labor intensive, ceramic tile walls for kitchens are burgeoning in popularity, and for good reason. Tile lends a natural air to increasingly high-tech kitchens, and its resistance to water, heat, and grease make it practical and long lasting. Tile can be installed on an entire wall, or it can be used as a design accent or to cover a small area that receives hard use, such as a backsplash. Tile may be required by local code around a commercial range or a wood-burning stove. For kitchen walls, choose a glazed vitreous or semivitreous tile; avoid tiles described as unglazed or nonvitreous.

Tiles cut from marble, granite, or slate, called dimensioned stone, can be used sparingly on walls if they are cut thin enough to adhere vertically.

The tile dealer will help you determine how much tile is needed—based on the square footage of the walls to be covered and the linear measurement of any areas requiring edging or trim tiles—and can provide the proper adhesive, grout, and tools as well.

Wood

The most typical use of wood as a kitchen wall finish is for wainscoting. Usually, tongue-and-groove boards are installed vertically along the bottom half of the wall and capped with trim at chair-rail height. Depending on the type of wood and finish you choose, this look can coordinate with themes as diverse as American country, French provincial, and Victorian. Kitchen wainscoting that continues into a dining area will visually tie the spaces together.

Of course, wood can be used as a wall finish throughout the kitchen, with a few practical requirements. Wood used near wet areas, such as a sink backsplash, must be coated front and back with a water-resistant sealer before applying a polyurethane or other synthetic finish; avoid latex paint. For easy cleanup, choose a smoothly milled, close-grained wood and apply a high-quality alkyd paint or urethane varnish.

Wood wall treatments are moderate to very expensive, but not difficult to install.

Continuing the countertop laminate on the backsplash provides both design rhythm and ease of maintenance in this contemporary kitchen.

Trim

In its simplest form, wood trim is used to finish the casings of doors and windows and for baseboards. Its original purpose was to conceal joints. But with imagination, wood trim can become a potent design feature in its own right. The style of trim—or the choice of no trim at all—will subtly influence the look of the entire kitchen. Trim can be used to tie together disparate kitchen elements and to create lines of sight that the eye follows. For example, a cornice molding applied at the top edge of the wall cabinets can be extended around the room as a picture rail; or window sills can be positioned and designed so that they continue as a handy backsplash ledge along the countertops. Integrating these details requires forethought. Now is the time to start thinking about the relationships among the various parts of your kitchen and how trim might pull them together.

Most trim is made from small-dimension lumber, such as 1 by 2s, and from inexpensive wood-molding stock, which comes in hundreds of decorative shapes.

Decorative trim doesn't have to be wood. Lightweight pressed-foam trim—often shaped to mimic intricate wood designs—is available in a variety of styles, is easy to cut, and is not difficult to install with a bit of practice. Ceramic tiles can be used to decorate windows or doors or to form an eye-catching chair or picture rail.

Wall Trim Treatments

DOORS

Efficient traffic patterns into and around the kitchen are enhanced by the placement and design of doors. The right door complements the style of the house as well as the kitchen. Energy efficiency and ease of maintenance are other worthwhile considerations.

Door Types

Standard doors for the exterior and interior come in prehung packages or can be built on site. Prehung door packages, which include the side jambs, the head jamb, and a door already mounted on hinges, are usually slightly more expensive than building your own jambs and mounting your own hinges, but the assembled units can save hours of painstaking work. When designing your floor plan, you must keep in mind the height, width, and swing clearance for every door. If you plan to purchase prehung packages, follow the manufacturer's specifications. When ordering a prehung package, you must specify whether the door will open from the right or left, whether it will swing in or out, and the width of the jamb (usually 4⅝ inches for wallboard walls and 5⅜ inches for plaster walls). If you buy your lockset before ordering the door, the manufacturer can drill the door to the lock specifications.

If you are not changing the location of the kitchen door, you can probably install a standard new door in the existing frame, with the following exceptions.

- If the old door is shorter than 80 inches, you'll have to cut down the new door; if the old door is taller than 7 feet, you'll have to order a custom-made door.
- If the new door has a different thickness, check the door-frame stops; if they are rabbeted into the jambs rather than nailed to the surface, you will have to replace the jambs to reposition the stops.
- If your kitchen door opens into the garage, most codes require a special solid-core door

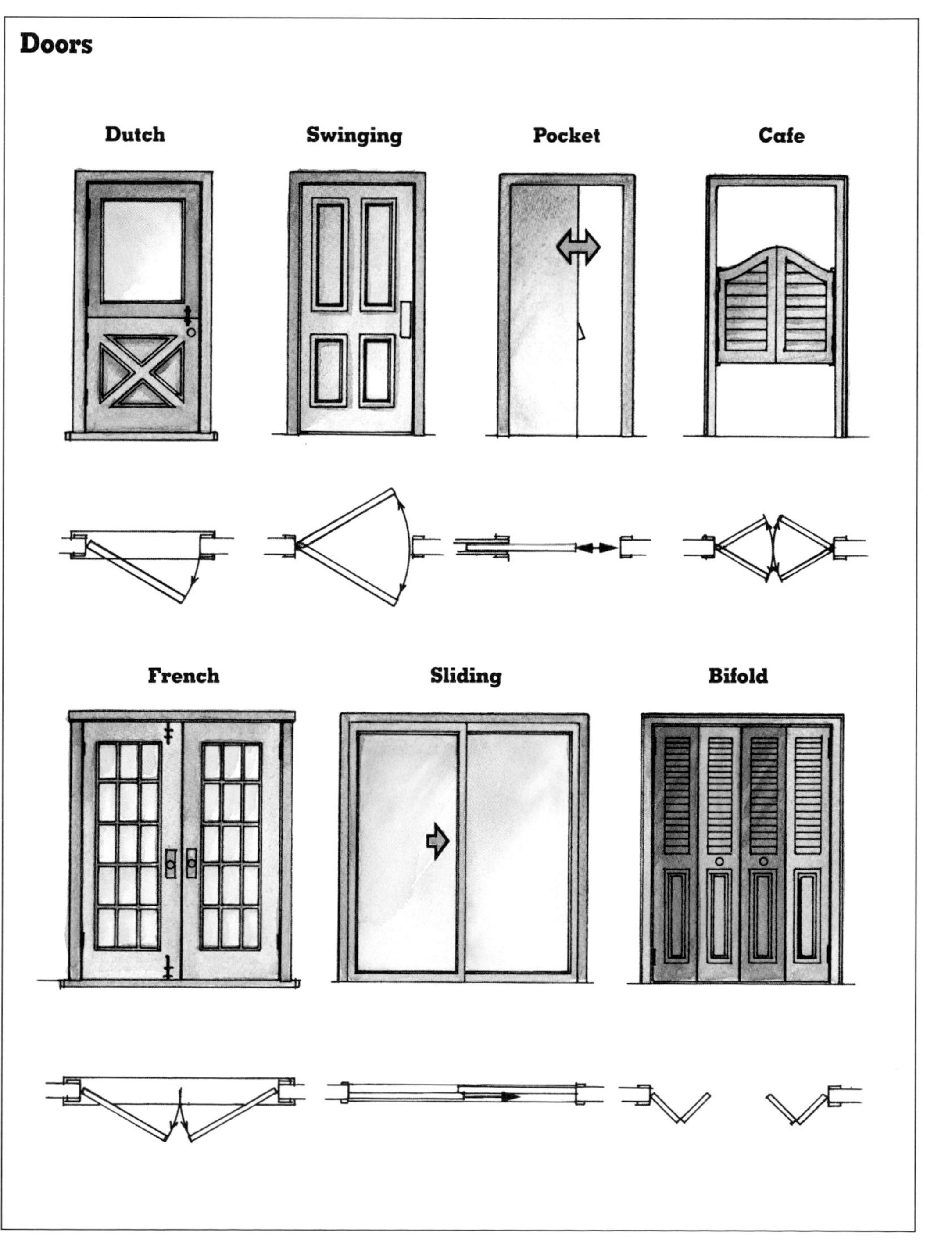

that is resistant to fire and the passage of fumes.

• If you are installing a door that is antique or otherwise one of a kind, expect to rebuild the frame to fit it.

Exterior Doors

Exterior doors are classified either as entry—the front door—or auxiliary—the side and back doors. The kitchen door is nearly always an auxiliary door. So long as there is an entry door at least 36 inches wide, most codes allow an auxiliary door to be 32 inches wide. However, wheelchair access requires a 36-inch width. Exterior doors are normally 1¾ inches thick and not less than 80 inches tall.

Exterior doors are a part of the weather seal of your home. You must ensure that they fit snugly and are properly weather-stripped. Some codes require that exterior doors swing outward; if you are changing the door location, be sure to check current codes.

Wood Panel

The most popular style, this solid-wood door has a stile-and-rail construction enclosing panels. The type of wood and panel shape can be adapted to any traditional-style kitchen. Wood doors are available in many wood species, can be stained or painted, and are naturally insulating. They can be trimmed to fit on all four sides and also come prehung.

Steel

Steel doors have a wood inner frame with a foam core encased in steel front and back. Styled to look like wood doors, they are usually painted. Steel doors are increasingly popular because of their security advantages and fire resistance. Their insulating qualities and tight fit make them an excellent choice for areas with severe weather; they're especially resistant to heat transmission. These doors must be purchased prehung or must have a new frame built for them because they cannot be trimmed.

Sliding Glass

Basically a wall-sized window, sliding glass doors are an attractive choice for a kitchen overlooking a patio, garden, or deck. They are sold in kits that include the panels, frame, and necessary hardware, and come in widths of 5 to 20 feet and heights from 6½ to 8 feet, with two, three, or four panels. The frames may be wood or aluminum. Wood is heavier and more expensive, but it insulates better; it also looks better, if the house windows are wood. Tempered shatterproof glass makes the door safer, and local codes may require it. Specify double-glazed glass, which effects quite an energy savings, in any but the mildest climate. The threshold of a sliding door must be kept scrupulously clean to operate properly, and the door usually requires a window treatment for privacy.

French

Also called double doors, French-style wood doors are almost always fully paned and are overtaking sliding glass doors in popularity for their window-wall effect. Clean-lined yet warm, French doors work well with most themes, from Colonial to Victorian to Palladian.

In a double door, or set, one door is called inactive. It has a strip along the edge, called an astral, and is flush-bolted top and bottom to the door frame when not open. The active door closes against the astral, preventing the doors from being jimmied apart. Most sets have 3-foot-wide doors, though narrower ones are also available. They are available prehung like a conventional door, and can be used as a main entrance.

Dutch

The traditional door of Holland, a Dutch door is cut in two horizontally, so the top half of the door can swing open independently. Dutch doors can be used as interior doors as well, and are useful when the kitchen adjoins a playroom: Children can be seen without getting underfoot. A Dutch door must be custom-made on site from a conventional panel door. It is sawed at the center-rail position, and two hinges are applied to each section. A ledge can be installed on the lower half. The top half is held shut by a flush bolt.

Interior Doors

Most kitchens are designed with an open traffic flow from the dining area or family room. But if your kitchen opens onto several rooms in the house, you'll need doors to keep the kitchen from being used as a hallway, and to provide privacy and quiet to those other areas. You'll probably also want a door on a kitchen pantry, utility room, or mud room. The swing of a conventional door can get in the way of cabinets and appliances, so consider cafe doors, bifold doors, or a pocket door for tight areas.

Interior doors normally measure 32 inches wide, but they are available as small as 24 inches wide, and must be 36 inches wide for wheelchair access. Standard height is 80 inches. The details of ordering, wall framing, and installation are similar to those for an exterior door, but an interior door is not weather-stripped and often will not have a threshold. For a doorless passageway, the wall is cut through and framed as though for a door installation, but then the edges are simply trimmed to finish it. This is also the wall preparation for swinging, bifold, and cafe doors.

Panel

Like its exterior counterparts, an interior panel door is a solid-wood, stile-and-rail door. As a special design touch, look for a door—new or used—that matches your cabinets; perhaps a beautiful old door of oak or pine with unique panel detail. You can trim the edges of the panel door to fit the existing frame. New panel doors are available in prehung packages and can be painted or stained.

Hollow-Core

Inexpensive hollow-core doors are typical in new houses. A hollow-core door has a flat surface of wood veneer appiied to a light wood-frame edging, with a stiffener such as cardboard honeycomb inside. It is light and easy to install, and should be used if necessary to coordinate with other doors in the house, or in a location where budget is more important than looks. Hollow-core doors come in a paint or stain grade and are available prehung. They can be trimmed only 1 inch in height and 2 inches in width.

Solid-core doors are a variation on this design. They have an interior of particleboard, and may be sheathed in a higher-quality veneer. They are heavier, stronger, and more fire-resistant than the hollow-core type and are required by some codes at furnace-room or garage entrances. Solid-core doors are more soundproof as well, and are therefore a sensible choice for a laundry or bathroom adjacent to the kitchen.

Swinging

A swinging door between the kitchen and dining room is a traditional convenience for a cook laden with heavy dishes, because the automatic closure keeps the kitchen private. Swinging doors are available in full-length and cafe versions. To prevent collisions, a full-length swinging door should have a small window at eye level, and is not recommended for families with small children. Any solid-wood door can be made into a swinging door by adding a spring-operated floor hinge and a top pivot, following the manufacturer's instructions.

Cafe doors, the swinging doors of Old West saloons, close only the midpart of the doorway, screening the kitchen but allowing people to see each other. These specialty doors swing on gravity-pivot hinges screwed to the side jambs and are suitable for a casual kitchen, particularly one with a southwestern theme.

Dutch doors can be used on the interior and exterior. The glass panel on the top half of this door allows a view of the backyard from the island cooking center. In the foreground are an under-counter microwave oven and an island cooktop. This kitchen is also pictured on pages 42 and 43.

Bifold

Folding doors come in a single- or double-door arrangement. When open, they do not project far, making them ideal space savers for closing off a small kitchen or for screening areas such as a laundry or pantry. Louver doors lend a casual look; the solid-wood panel style is dressier. Bifold doors are installed with pivot hinges on the side jambs, and usually have a track at the top and bottom for the door-guide pins. Widths range from 24 inches to 6 feet or more.

Pocket

Popular in the Victorian era, a pocket door slides into the wall entirely. Closed, it walls off the kitchen completely; opened, it makes two rooms into one. Glass-paneled pocket doors allow in light and views while shutting out drafts and noise. The pocket frame is available as a kit. A conventional panel or hollow-core door up to 3 feet wide hangs from brackets in an overhead track or on the door edge; a pair of pocket frames can be installed for a double door. As existing wall sheathing must be removed and a doorway framed, this project is easiest with a new wall. The portion of the wall that houses the pocket door must not contain pipes, wires, ducts, or any other utility.

WINDOWS

Striking the balance between limited wall space and a desire for view and light is a matter of choosing the placement and design of windows and skylights. Airflow and emergency access are considerations when deciding whether windows are to be fixed or openable. Specialty window glass can add dramatic dimension to any kitchen.

Window Types

Like exterior doors, windows have three purposes. One function is to admit light and views while protecting against weather and dust. The second is to provide an exit in an emergency. The third is to enhance the design. Windows should have a look that complements the design of the house and kitchen. Consider all three purposes as you decide on the kinds of windows you want for your new kitchen.

There are so many styles—and manufacturers making slightly different versions of the same window—that the big problem is deciding what type you want. Familiarize yourself with the key aspects of different kinds of windows, both their qualities and their limitations, and then examine all the windows available from suppliers before you make your choices.

All window types are available prefabricated. Standard windows are originally installed with flanges to protect the opening in the exterior wall from leaks. So-called replacement windows, on the other hand, are designed to slide into an existing window frame. These work out quicker and cheaper because they save construction costs. Use the original window frames wherever your kitchen design permits. Ask the window dealer whether a prefabricated window that fits your existing frame is available. Most windows come with built-in screens. When shopping, check that the screen is sturdy and convenient to remove.

The considerations for opening an exterior wall for a window are the same as for an exterior door (see page 48). The window manufacturer will specify the rough-opening size you need. Installing a new window in an existing opening is simple. If the opening must be enlarged, keep in mind while designing that lowering the original sill plate is easy, but raising the header is a substantial structural change.

Frame Materials

Windows are framed with aluminum, wood, or plastic. The different materials affect cost, looks, and energy efficiency. Check the energy statistics when you comparison shop.

Aluminum windows come with or without thermal breaks, which encase the exterior of the frame and minimize the transmission of heat or cold. You'll never need to paint these frames, but the color selection is limited.

Metal frames without thermal breaks transmit cold and heat, which may lead to condensation problems. They are durable if the exterior is vinyl-clad or painted regularly to prevent rust.

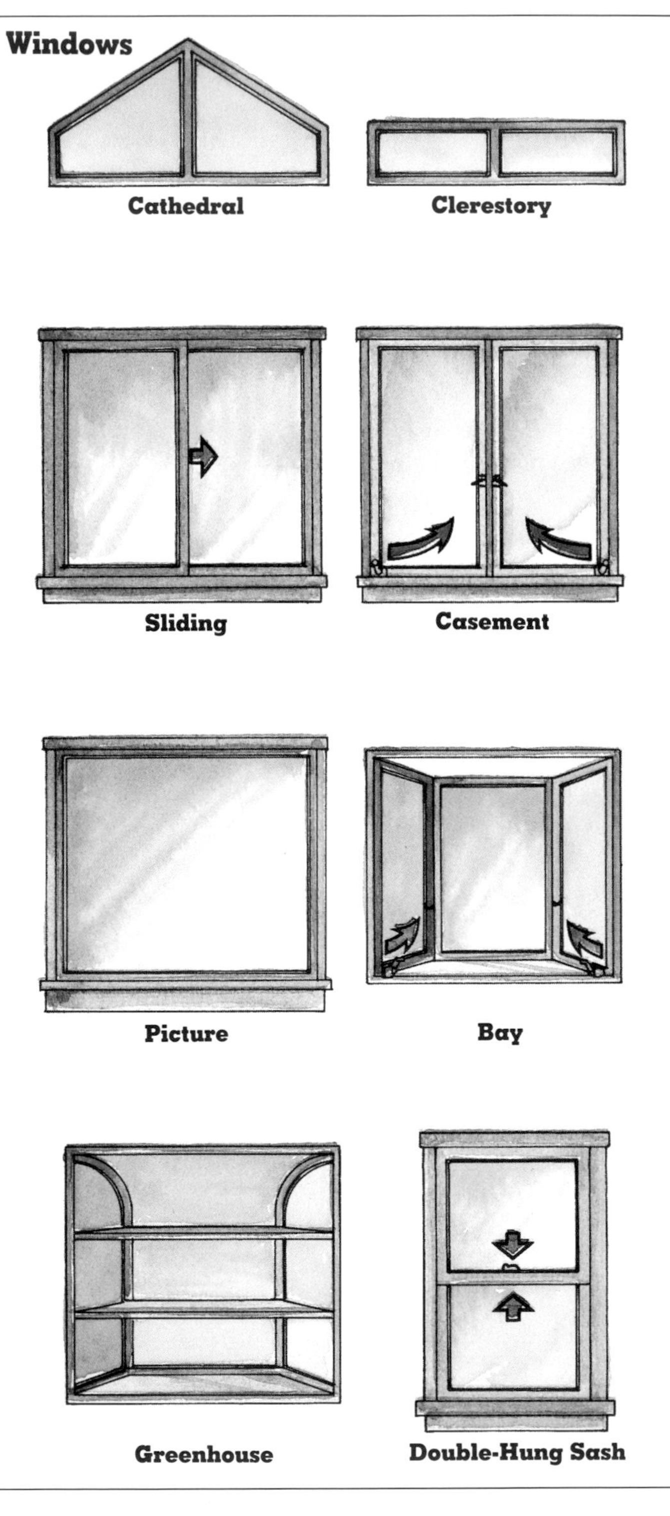

Traditional wood frames have excellent insulating qualities and seal tighter than metal frames. However, a skilled carpenter must install them, and they must be painted regularly.

Clad-wood frames are factory-covered with protective vinyl on the exterior in a wide variety of colors, so no painting is required. In extreme cold, however, vinyl is brittle and may crack. Many clad-wood frames are left unclad on the interior side so they can be finished in keeping with the kitchen style.

Plastic window frames are usually the least expensive, but don't hold up as well as other materials under heavy use and come in limited styles.

Fixed Windows

Decorative windows that do not open are perfectly suited to the kitchen. These windows can be custom-made, but the hundreds of prefabricated ones anticipate nearly every design need and are much less expensive. Fixed windows are installed like other prefabricated windows.

Greenhouse

Also called a garden window, this popular style admits light for plants on three sides and from the top, while also creating a shelf for them. Though considered a fixed window, some have a pane or two that open for ventilation. A western exposure is too intense for most plants, but a greenhouse window will make the most of a northern exposure. It looks attractive above a sink, and at countertop level is convenient for watering. Many prefabricated variations are available; some are inexpensive—and look it. Because the window protrudes, it is especially important that it complement the architectural style of the house in order not to look stuck on as an afterthought. Choose double-glazed glass, which prevents condensation, a common problem with greenhouse windows.

Bay

Similar in concept to a greenhouse window, a bay window is usually the focal point of a room. It consists of a large picture window with a narrower window on each side angled back toward the wall. A bow window is similar but is shaped as one large curving surface. A bay window may take up the entire end wall of a breakfast nook, vastly enlarging the perceived space, increasing the light, and even providing seating. Make sure the view outside is worthy of

A view from the kitchen sink is an oft-desired feature. An angled bow (above) and a square greenhouse (below) each do the job.

such a grand frame, or install colored or stained glass to screen an unwanted view. Be sure that the bay window coordinates with and doesn't overwhelm the house.

Bay windows are expensive and come in limited sizes. Even prefabricated ones may need to be partly assembled on site by the installer. If you decide a bay is the window you want, consult closely with the manufacturer to prepare the wall and roof properly.

Picture

A standard of gracious suburban living, the picture window is a must if the surrounding outdoors is lovely to look at. Simply a pane of glass in a frame, it is easy—if somewhat unwieldy—to install, and is inexpensive compared with many specialty windows. As with any large expanse of glass, it should be double-glazed, except in a very mild climate. Consider the location of the sun in summer and winter when designing for a picture window; intense light, such as a western exposure, can be unpleasant and hot. Follow the manufacturer's recommendations for rough-framing the wall; the large expanse of glass may require extra bracing. In most neighborhoods, a large window usually calls for a substantial window treatment for privacy, another design factor—as well as expense—to consider.

Decorative Glass

Once a traditional—and somewhat ponderous—look, today's decorative glass windows have come into their own as a practical, interesting design element. Practical, because in this day of zero-lot-line and communal building, they offer privacy as well as luxury. Decorative glass—stained, colored, leaded, frosted, or textured—is an excellent design choice for a window that gets plenty of light but has a poor view.

Another alternative is an overlay. This thin sheet can be applied to any window for the effect of stained, frosted, or textured glass. It is stronger and more weather resistant than real specialty glass, and you can design any motif to complement your kitchen. Ask the overlay dealer for a catalog of examples.

Including some openable windows in a bow arrangement provides ventilation as well as views. These multiple panes match those in the French doors pictured on page 29.

Clerestory and Cathedral

Unusual options for window placement are especially useful in the kitchen, where wall space is in short supply. Clerestory windows allow for extra light and privacy and are installed in a narrow band along the ceiling or in the wall over the cabinets. Windows that fit such a space are available prefabricated. Although they are short, their width requires a specially reinforced header.

Cathedral windows fill the triangular space where a wall meets a vaulted ceiling. These are usually custom-made to fit the space, with or without a finish frame. Consider this type of window as a source of light if you decide to vault the kitchen ceiling.

Some manufacturers offer triangular shapes and fanlike multipaneled windows, which can become the focal point of a kitchen wall.

Openable Windows

Windows that open for ventilation are particularly necessary in the kitchen, where cooking produces heat, fumes, steam, and, inevitably, the occasional smoke. Of the many different window mechanisms, most are one of two basic types: sliders and swingers.

Sliding

A sliding window has a frame that moves in tracks. The two types of sliders are sash windows, which open vertically, and gliding windows, which open horizontally. Sliding windows open to a maximum of only 50 percent of the window area, but they seal out the weather better than swingers.

Sash windows, the traditional over-and-under type, are available double-hung, in which both panes slide independently, and single-hung, in which only the bottom pane moves. The glass area may be left plain, or it can be divided by mullions into various panes. A gliding window has sashes that slide horizontally in tracks at the top and bottom.

Swinging

A swinging window has a geared mechanism that pivots outward to open. Swingers include awning windows, in which the bottom edge pivots outward; hoppers, in which the top edge pivots inward; and casement windows, which swing or crank open sideways on hinges. Swinging windows are suitable for mild and warm climates for several reasons: The window area opens 100 percent and, in the case of awning windows, the panes deflect rain (and, if tinted, sun as well). In general, swinging windows, because they protrude when open, tend to get dirty faster than sliders.

FLOORING

Floors have the toughest job of any kitchen surface. They are expected to stand up to traffic and spills yet look lovely again with the swipe of a damp mop. A surprising variety of flooring materials is available, many designed with kitchens in mind, that will meet this challenge—and beautifully to boot.

Structural Changes

What is called the floor is really just a protective and decorative surface treatment. Underneath, a sandwich of construction materials, called the subfloor, supports the house and provides a firm, smooth surface for the finish floor. Most homes have either a concrete slab or wood-frame subfloor.

Concrete Subfloor

A concrete slab is strong and stable. It provides an excellent foundation for rigid flooring materials, such as ceramic tile, and flexible materials, such as resilient sheet flooring. Some wood flooring products, such as parquet tiles, can be glued directly to concrete; others, such as wood strip flooring, require a "sleeper floor" of plywood and 2 by 4s as a nailing surface. Note that this raises the floor surface by more than 2 inches—a difficult side effect to design around. For any flooring, the slab must be dry; if yours has a moisture-accumulation problem, consult with a specialist to correct it before proceeding. Check the existing finish floor for clues, such as loose tiles, lifted seams, or bubbles.

Wood Subfloor

A wood-frame subfloor has a smooth layer of plywood nailed directly to the joists. It is usually topped by felt paper, then covered with tongue-and-groove strip flooring or other type of flooring material. To accept a ceramic-tile floor, the subfloor must be very rigid; this normally requires installation of additional plywood or tile backer board acceptable for floor use. For a very heavy floor, such as stone, the joists themselves must be reinforced, usually by blocking between them. A smooth, even surface of floorboards may be left in place as the subfloor for most materials, but must be overlaid with ⅜- or ½-inch plywood.

Remember that for any additional subfloor layer, you must add its thickness to the finish floor height. This will affect your kitchen design in terms of floor-to-counter measurement, light switch placement, threshold transition, and other small but significant details.

Existing Finish Floors

Check your existing floor for water damage, especially around the sink and appliances, and plan on repairing it. Any high points in the floor must be sanded down, and low points filled, before a new floor can be laid.

In most cases, a new finish floor can be installed directly over existing flooring if it is solid and the subfloor underneath is healthy. Of course, carpeting must be removed, and very cushioned resilient flooring is too giving a surface for a subfloor. If you suspect that the existing floor might contain asbestos, the safest course is to cover it. If it must be taken up, call a professional service specializing in asbestos removal.

Design Considerations

A multitude of kitchen flooring materials and finishes offer a range of looks as varied as for the rest of the house. Your choice will be a highly personal one. Remember, with some effort several finish floors can be combined effectively within a single kitchen.

Looks are not everything. Keep in mind that you may be on your feet in the kitchen for several hours each day. This fact makes the "feel" of the floor, both real and perceived, relatively significant. Flooring materials range from cool to warm and are hard or yielding. In choosing flooring, consider your climate and life-style. Do you go barefoot indoors? What feels good against your stocking feet? Do you have toddlers who will undoubtedly tumble on the floor?

The kitchen floor plan and the type of anticipated activity centers have an impact on the appropriate finish floor. If the kitchen includes an eating area, the type of floor beneath the table should be easy to clean. If the room contains a laundry center, consider the potential noise as well as how water from an overflowing washing machine would affect the floor.

You must also think about traffic patterns when choosing the finish flooring. If the room contains an exterior door, people will be passing through the kitchen directly from outdoors, which means that dirt and water will be tracked onto the kitchen floor.

Aesthetic considerations are fundamental to the future enjoyment of the room. The color, texture, and pattern of the flooring should coordinate—without competing—with the overall design concept of the kitchen. This takes some forethought, because the floor is the largest unbroken surface in the room. A common mistake is to choose a patterned sheet flooring based on a small sample; once on the floor, however, the pattern repeat becomes overwhelming.

It is also possible to unintentionally introduce pattern into a room by your choice of materials. For example, a neutral ceramic-tile floor can set up an unanticipated grid pattern if the grout is a contrasting color.

A unique floor pattern can be an exciting design element; to emphasize it, keep your countertops and wallcoverings very simple. Texture works the same way. A rough slate floor is best complemented by smooth, simple surfaces.

The most basic maintenance feature for a kitchen floor is washability. If you have children and pets, the floor must stand up to a daily mopping with floor cleaner; choose a high-quality resilient sheet or tile. If your household is more sedate, you must still ask how much maintenance is acceptable for you. Is the mellow appearance of an oiled wood floor worth regular stripping and waxing? It may well be. When shopping for floor coverings, be sure to ask what maintenance will be required.

Wood

Wood floors in the kitchen have had a surge of popularity for several reasons: Kitchens are now seen as rooms for living, not just using. Modern finishes, such as polyurethane and waterproof sealers, make wood floors practical in a hardworking environment. Oak is by far the most popular and practical wood flooring for the home. It is very durable and is much cheaper than maple—the hardest surface. Pine is also popular for its traditional country roots, but it dents more easily and is more porous, so for the kitchen it must be finished carefully. Most wood flooring is tongue-and-groove strips 2¼ inches wide, blind-nailed to the subfloor through the tongues. Choose Clear or Select grades for a light, natural finish; Select or #1 Common will do for a stained floor. The subfloor should be ⅝-inch or thicker plywood, clean and level.

Measure the square footage of the floor and allow 10 percent extra for waste. Hardwood floors usually stop just 1 inch beyond the toe kick of floor cabinets, saving some cost. Remember to extend the floor under the refrigerator, range, and any other movable appliance.

Resilients

This versatile, durable flooring material was designed with kitchens in mind, but is used throughout the house. Resilients are available as sheet flooring and tiles. Resilient sheet flooring is often misnamed linoleum; linoleum is a different product that was used extensively on kitchen floors for many years but is rarely used today.

Both sheets and tiles are inexpensive, waterproof, easy to clean, and, of course, resilient underfoot. Both types are available in myriad colors, patterns, and textures.

The predominant consideration when choosing resilient flooring is quality. Choose a medium or heavy gauge with a thick "wear layer"—the protective topcoat over the pattern. A thick cushion backing is

A fancifully painted floor is a perfect visual balance to the spectacular use of clerestory windows in this kitchen. The paint effect was achieved by applying a colored stain on a wood floor, stenciling the patterns, and then using two coats of polyurethane finish to protect the delicate design.

quieter, more comfortable, and more forgiving if you drop something breakable. Higher quality means higher price, but it's a worthwhile investment.

Most sheet flooring is available in rolls 6 and 12 feet wide. Tiles are usually 12-inch squares.

More than any other flooring, resilient requires an absolutely smooth, clean subfloor; every pit and crack will show through and eventually cause uneven wear. If you cannot perfect the subfloor, choose another finish floor surface.

Ceramic Tile

A highly durable flooring, ceramic tile offers any look from rustic to ultramodern, and new glazes provide deep, saturated colors. A tile floor is relatively expensive, but the variety of sizes and colors allows you to express yourself by creating one-of-a-kind patterns and color combinations to suit your kitchen. Coordinating tile on the countertops and backsplash lends a unified effect, but too much tile can be overwhelming. Be sure you choose a tile specified for use on the floor; wall tile is not strong enough, and a slick designer glaze can be dangerous. Keep in mind that a tile floor remains cool, which is a plus or a drawback depending on your life-style and climate.

Ceramic floor tiles are usually square or octagonal, in any size from 1 inch, called mosaics, to 18 inches but 4- to 6-inch tiles are typical. Mosaics and intricately shaped arabesque tiles are arranged in groups on a mesh backing for easier installation. The subfloor must be smooth, rigid plywood or tile backer board.

Dimensioned Stone

Marble, slate, and granite come in thin, polished 12-inch squares called dimensioned-stone tiles. These natural products are an expensive floor treatment, but offer a stunning, elegant effect, worth the cost for dressing up a tiny jewel of a kitchen or for a kitchen that opens directly onto a formal entertaining area. The veining in every tile is unique; try to view as large a sample as possible, and remember that a strong pattern will rivet the eye. A stone floor may make itself the focal point of your kitchen. Coordinating stone floors and countertops can be effective, but as with ceramic tile, don't allow stone to become overwhelming.

Kitchen Carpet

Use caution when choosing carpet for the kitchen. Kitchen carpet offers unsurpassed comfort underfoot, excellent noise reduction, and warmth; it also camouflages small surface flaws in a subfloor. But it absorbs liquids, may stain, and over time accumulates ground-in dirt and food particles. It cannot be wet-mopped; it must be vacuumed and periodically shampooed. Carpet is well suited for a breakfast nook or a social area away from the food-preparation and cleanup centers. A small pattern can help disguise stains. The carpeting used for kitchens has a short, dense loop pile of nylon on a foam backing and doesn't require a pad. It comes in 6- and 12-foot-wide rolls.

Edge Treatments

Almost any finish floor requires some sort of trim around its edges, which seals the joint where floor meets wall and protects the wall when the floor is washed. Trim set flush with the wall is called a baseboard. The area recessed under cabinets is called the toe kick. Both are fundamental design elements, which will strongly influence the look of the kitchen.

Wood

A wood baseboard treatment is appropriate for any floor. The baseboard may be a single curved piece, called clamshell molding, or may consist of several fancy moldings applied to a 1-by board for a formal look. Traditionally, a shoe molding, or quarter-round, applied at floor level, is the finishing touch, but this seems to be going out of style. Wood baseboards can be stained to match the kitchen floor or cabinets, and are available in hardwoods.

Vinyl

Vinyl cove is a practical, washable edge treatment for resilient vinyl floors and for toe kicks. Its use with other, more expensive types of flooring, however, will cheapen their effect. Purchase vinyl cove by the linear foot, and attach it with the same adhesive used for resilient flooring. Some vinyl cove has a peel-and-stick backing. Vinyl cove is bent around corners rather than cut.

Tile

Ceramic border tiles are an attractive, practical, washable edge treatment for ceramic floors. Tiles can also be used effectively to edge other flooring materials, especially if the edge-treatment tiles are coordinated with countertop and wall tiles. For edge treatments, specify tiles with one rounded, or bullnose, edge at the top. The edge tiles can be continued along the toe kick.

Thresholds

A threshold serves as a transition where unlike flooring materials meet at a doorway; it can also soften the contrast between different floor levels. At an exterior door, it helps seal the bottom of the entrance. A threshold is not needed in a doorway where the same flooring material is continued into the next room unless there is a seam.

Thresholds are made of wood, metal, or—in rare instances—stone. Wood is used to match a wood floor, especially where one type of wood flooring joins another of a different layout pattern or species. A wood threshold is cut to length and nailed to the floor.

Interior metal thresholds are thin, flat aluminum bars that finish off the edges of vinyl flooring or thin carpet. These are cut or scored and snapped to length and usually come with tacks for attaching. They are available in several colors. Exterior-door metal thresholds are more substantial and may have built-in weather stripping. These are cut to fit and then screwed into place.

A reducer strip is an additional threshold treatment, useful when a new floor is installed over an old one.

CEILINGS

Many kitchen-remodel jobs require that you strip the existing ceiling to the joists in order to upgrade the wiring. This is a perfect opportunity to rethink the ceiling design. Vaulting the ceiling, exposing the beams, or adding a skylight will brighten the room and make it seem larger.

Existing Ceilings

If you are moving any walls, or stripping the substrate from the studs, it is most practical to go ahead and remove the ceiling surface as well. Even if the walls will stay in place, consider replacing the ceiling if any of the following conditions is met.

- The ceiling is made of plaster and lath that is cracked or sagging.
- The wallboard is uneven or has obvious joints, nails, or tape.
- The ceiling was water damaged at one time.
- You plan to redesign the kitchen lighting.
- You want to add insulation between the ceiling and roof.

If the ceiling is sound and its configuration fits the planned kitchen design, consider yourself lucky and by all means keep it in place.

Visual Tricks

The ceiling configuration can be altered using visual tricks. Lower a too-high ceiling by painting it a darker color than the walls; papering it to match the walls; applying a wallcovering border or a picture-rail molding to the wall about a foot below the ceiling and painting the area above it darker; or installing a suspended ceiling. A suspended ceiling is a simple network of metal framing strips that can hold ceiling panels and luminous fluorescent panels for improved lighting. The old ceiling, above the lowered one, may be unattractive or even damaged, so long as it is structurally sound.

To make a ceiling look higher, paint it a lighter color than the walls, using semigloss rather than gloss paint, install wallcovering with a vertical pattern, and avoid horizontal trim near the ceiling. A ceiling that is too low can feel oppressive and make the kitchen hot. If the ceiling is lower than 8 feet, strongly consider raising it structurally to feel comfortable and to make it proportional to

Skylights placed between the rafters of this vaulted ceiling allow for stargazing during midnight snacks. Raising the ceiling increases the perceived square footage of any room.

Cabinet Top Treatments

Open Soffit

Flush Soffit Box

Held-back Soffit Box

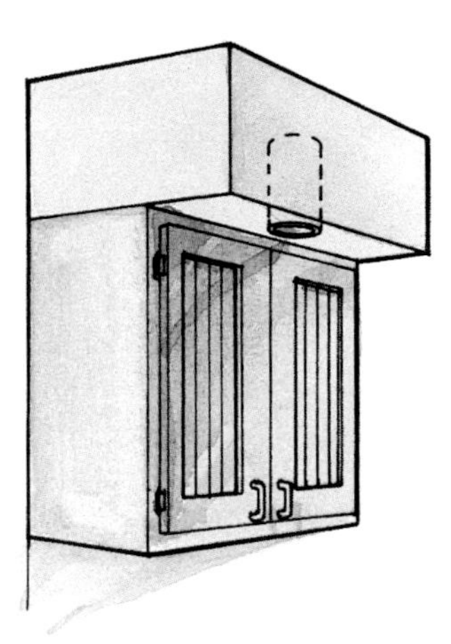

Extended Soffit Box With Lighting

modern cabinets and appliances. Local code may require a higher ceiling if you do any remodeling. If an existing suspended ceiling is lower than 8 feet, remove it and install recessed lighting in the structural ceiling instead.

Ceiling Configurations

With floor area at a premium in new-house construction, architects and designers have discovered the ceiling as a design element. Modern ceilings may be vaulted, coffered, or cathedral style. All of these terms refer to a ceiling that extends to the roof rafters, or nearly so, rather than running flat at the horizontal joists. Obviously, in order to accomplish this, the kitchen must not be situated below living space. Although extending the ceiling this way does not add square footage to the room, it does add cubic footage to the interior space, introducing light and air—in short, breathing room.

Redesigning the ceiling may be the most dramatic way you can alter the atmosphere of your kitchen. On the practical side, extending the ceiling upward makes room for more windows and storage space and draws heat away from the cooking center.

Soffit Areas

The space between the tops of wall cabinets and the ceiling is the soffit area. One treatment is to leave it open and use it for display or storage space, although this becomes a dustcatcher that may drive a neatnik crazy. Another idea is to extend the cabinets all the way to the ceiling, adding considerable storage space, albeit difficult to reach. Often, the soffit is filled with a framed box, which is covered with wallboard and finished to match the surrounding walls. The box can be built flush with the cabinets, held back halfway for a display area, or extended over them. Often an extended box is wired to contain recessed light fixtures that aim cones of light on specific work centers.

Skylights

Since the walls in a typical kitchen are mostly taken up by built-ins, the ceiling is a sensible place to look for window space. A well-placed skylight can provide all the light a kitchen needs during the day. In fact, it provides much more light than a window of the same size, and high-quality units can be extremely energy efficient.

A skylight is installed on the roof, either with its own built-in flashing or else set on a built-up curb. To keep costs down, make sure that there is nothing structural in the attic to get in the way of the skylight. Also, purchase a skylight made to fit the spacing between the rafters, usually 16 or 24 inches on center, although wider skylights are available.

Some styles open and close for ventilation, either manually, with a remote control, or with a time-controlled sensor.

PLUMBING

The structural survey familiarized you with the existing plumbing system in your house. Depending on the locations and types of appliances and plumbing fixtures planned for the new kitchen, changes or additions to this system may be necessary. This might also be an opportune time to upgrade the system with modern, efficient materials.

System Requirements

The basic plumbing in a kitchen is located in the cleanup center, which usually consists of the main sink, garbage disposer, and dishwasher. A set of supply pipes for hot and cold water, and a drainpipe serve this sink. A branch drain may connect the drainpipe to the main drain of the house. If the sink is far from the main soil stack (the upper extension of the main drain, which vents it through the roof), it will have its own secondary vent pipe extending up the wall and through the roof. The dishwasher and disposer drain into the trap and drainpipe of the main sink. Water supply pipes for other kitchen fixtures and appliances usually branch off of the main sink pipes. Gas piping uses materials and techniques similar to simple plumbing.

Locating plumbing fixtures in the kitchen depends on three primary considerations:

- The location and accessibility of existing plumbing
- The requirements of the local plumbing code
- The ease of fitting new plumbing pipes into the existing house structure

Adding a second sink or moving the present one to another wall requires additional plumbing. However, shifting fixtures just a few inches can be done by connecting extenders to the existing pipes. Always consult local codes for exact requirements prior to making adjustments and adding appliances to an existing system.

The DWV System

The existing arrangement of the drain, waste, and vent (DWV) system may influence the new design; plumbing codes are quite strict about such details as pipe size, angle, and length of run, so you may prefer to leave fixtures where they are to avoid costly in-wall restructuring.

All plumbing fixtures must be vented through the roof. Some fixtures have vent pipes that return to the main stack, or they may vent independently. When making decisions regarding plumbing changes, remember that the bulk of the expense is in gaining access to pipes and running new ones through the existing house structure. Adding a new vent pipe requires installing it in an existing wall, which can be complicated, or building a new wall for it—a thicker wall made of 2 by 6s, called a wet wall. For any changes such as these, check the projected locations of the new pipes to make sure no critical components of the house are in the way.

However, don't let the existing DWV system curtail your creativity, so long as your changes are legal. Instead, let your ingenuity solve the problems. For example, if you want a window over the sink, the vent pipe can't extend straight up through it; but by using a pair of 45-degree bends you can send the pipe up along one side of the window, and still satisfy the code.

The rules for water supply lines are somewhat simpler. The size of the pipes—and what they are made of—is specified by code, based on such details as the type of fixture and the length of the pipe.

Pipe Types

Depending on the age of the house, the existing DWV pipes are probably made of cast iron and galvanized steel, and the supply pipes of galvanized steel, rigid copper, and some plastic pipe. Steel pipe is not recommended for new plumbing; copper or plastic can easily be added to a steel system.

Accepted cautiously when it was first introduced, plastic pipe has become the material of

Remodeling is a good time to consider updating the plumbing system to include a water-purifying feature like this one.

choice for plumbing remodeling, and is now allowed by most codes. However, check your local code before using it. It is lightweight, somewhat to very flexible, and the joints are simply glued together.

Different types of plastic pipe, each with a unique chemical formulation, are suited to different uses. For the DWV system, ABS (acrylonitrile-butadiene-styrene) pipe is recommended. For the supply system, choose PVC (polyvinyl chloride) pipe, or the newer CPVC (chlorinated polyvinyl chloride) pipe, which is better for hot-water lines. PVC pipe can also be used in the DWV system. PB (polybutylene) pipe can be used for supply lines in some localities. It is joined with compression fittings, not glued.

The fittings used for any type of pipe must be of the same material as the pipe. Cement used to join plastic pipe must be formulated for that plastic. In addition, most codes specify that pipes of different plastics cannot be mixed in the same system. Plastic pipe comes in the same nominal sizes as metal pipe, and has all the same fittings. A variety of adapter fittings connect plastic pipe to a metal system.

If codes do not allow plastic pipe, or you prefer not to use it for the supply lines, the best bet is copper. Copper pipe is corrosion resistant and fairly light. It can be bent around corners, requiring fewer joints. However, copper pipe is much more expensive than plastic.

Appliance Requirements

Plumbing is required for the sink, garbage disposer, and dishwasher. You may also have a second sink, a washing machine, a water heater, and a refrigerator with an ice maker and water dispenser, each of which has plumbing requirements. Gas ranges, clothes dryers, and water heaters also require gas piping.

Some plumbing aspects for individual fixtures and appliances are dictated by code; others are determined by the location of the item in the overall kitchen design. Every fixture or appliance should have a cutoff valve, also called a supply stop, on an accessible part of each supply pipe, so that water to it can be turned off independently for service. Each supply pipe should also have an air chamber, a vertical extension that is capped at the top. This prevents water hammering when the water is turned off.

Sinks

All sinks require hot and cold supply pipes with cutoff valves that connect to flexible tubing in the faucet assembly. The drainpipe requires a P-trap. A double sink requires only one trap, which can be located below one of the sinks or centered between them.

Garbage Disposers

Each disposer fits onto the drain outlet of the sink. On a single sink, the drainpipe for both sink and disposer exits the disposer, then forms a P-trap. On a double sink, the drainpipe and P-trap exit the nondisposer side, and the disposer drains into them via an extension pipe that enters the drainpipe above the P-trap. The connection between the extension pipe and the drainpipe is a directional tee, which helps keep disposer contents from backing up into the sink.

Dishwasher

The supply line for the dishwasher is ⅜-inch flexible copper tubing. This can feed directly off the sink hot-water supply pipe with a tee fitting, but it should have its own cutoff valve. The drain hose from the dishwasher is connected to the sink drainpipe above the trap. It is routed through a high loop—the drain hose must rise at least to the level of the top of the dishwasher to prevent back flow. At this point it should have an air-gap assembly installed on the sink ledge.

Refrigerator

An automatic ice maker or water dispenser normally uses ¼-inch copper tubing, but refer to the manufacturer's specifications. This is connected to a cold-water supply pipe, usually under the sink, with a tee fitting and a cutoff valve. If the sink supply pipe is too far away, check in the wall behind the refrigerator, or under the floor, for another cold-water supply pipe.

Clothes Washer

This will probably be the only appliance in the kitchen with its own supply pipes for both hot and cold water. Each pipe ends in a hose bib, a type of faucet onto which the washer hose is screwed. The inlet valves in the washer close immediately once it is full; to avoid damage from water hammering, the supply pipes must be fitted with 18-inch air chambers or with shock absorbers. Unless the washer drain hose empties into a laundry tub, it requires a drain standpipe. This should be about 3 feet tall and have a P-trap at the bottom, within 18 inches of the floor.

Water Heater

Every water heater requires a cold-water supply pipe of ¾ inch, with a cutoff valve on it. The exit pipe for the hot water may be ½ inch or ¾ inch. A temperature/pressure-relief valve on the body of the heater or on the exit pipe will have a vertical drainpipe. A gas heater will have a gas pipe with an easily accessible cutoff valve. If allowed by code, gas and water pipes may have flexible hoses, which make it easier to position the heater.

Gas Lines

There are local variations in the codes relating to gas service. Check the requirements in your area before you decide how to install a gas appliance. Generally, gas lines are galvanized or ungalvanized steel or heavy-gauge copper pipe, and must have an easily reached cutoff valve positioned near the appliance. A permit is required for any new gas lines, and the system must be inspected and tested before it can be turned on.

ELECTRICAL

If your remodeling plans include improved lighting, new appliances, or more receptacles, changes need to be made to the electrical system. Decide on the number, location, amperage, and voltage of the individual kitchen circuits. Then determine whether the existing service will be adequate. You may need to upgrade the service-entrance box.

Determining Needs

In many locations, any changes or additions to kitchen wiring will require that the whole electrical system be brought up to current code. This could mean rewiring the entire house, including adding extra receptacles in every room. Check local codes for requirements or consult an electrical inspector, and familiarize yourself with the regulations in the *National Electrical Code* (*NEC*). Local regulations may also restrict the kinds of electrical work you are permitted to do yourself.

In general, a house with a modern, well-equipped kitchen will benefit from a 200-ampere, 240-volt electrical service (the voltage needed to run a range or clothes dryer). This is called a three-wire service: Two 120-volt hot wires provide electricity, and a third wire completes the circuit. The amperage represents the maximum volume of electricity that is available to the system at one time.

You may be able to get away without an expensive upgrade if you already have a modern three-wire, 240-volt service of at least 100 amps. This provides 24,000 watts of power, considered the bare minimum for a typical home. If the appliances and circuits planned for the new kitchen will not require more wattage than what is presently used, and the existing service performs adequately, it is probably sufficient. However, do not shortchange yourself on electricity. It is better to upgrade the service while you have the permit and the opportunity than to suffer later with insufficient power or too few receptacles.

Circuits

The parts used in electrical work are simple and inexpensive, although their sizes, materials, and configurations are carefully controlled by code.

If your kitchen remodel requires opening the walls anyway, it is actually smarter to give your dreams free rein and upgrade the electrical service to the maximum. Wiring is the most economical major improvement to make and it is easy and methodical to do.

A kitchen has very specific minimum-circuit requirements but, of course, you can add any other circuits that will make the kitchen more convenient.

Once you've determined the electrical appliances you want in your new kitchen and the number and location of new receptacles, calculate, with the help of the *NEC* and local code guidelines, the additional amperage these will require. Compare the result to the amperage of the existing electrical service. If the projected amperage exceeds what's currently available, upgrade the service at the service-entrance panel.

If the service-entrance panel doesn't need to be upgraded, but space is tight, try adding half-size wafer breakers. Alternatively, consider installing a subpanel for just the kitchen circuits. Although a subpanel provides space for more circuits, it does not increase the overall amperage of house electrical service.

Receptacles

Receptacles may be either 120 or 240 volt, and have outlets for two- or three-pronged plugs of various configurations and amperages. Major appliances, such as ranges and clothes dryers, have plugs that require a specific style of electrical receptacle. Combination switch-receptacles are also available. Switches and receptacles must have the same amperage and voltage rating as their circuit.

An electrical box is required for every receptacle, switch, light fixture, built-in appliance, and wherever else wire connections are made.

As a general rule, receptacles over counters are located no more than 4 feet apart, with a receptacle over any counter wider than 12 inches. They are usually 42 inches from the floor, but plan their location to fit the design, especially if you are planning to tile the walls or backsplash.

Although your kitchen will have specific requirements, be sure to include the following often-forgotten receptacles:

- Inside an appliance garage
- For a gas range with electric features
- For a hood/vent with electric features
- For a microwave oven at use height
- One 2 feet from the floor for the refrigerator
- One 14 inches from the floor for a floor buffer or vacuum cleaner

GFCI

Many codes require GFCI (ground fault circuit interrupter) protection around kitchen sinks and other wet areas. The GFCI will shut off the power instantly before electricity can be grounded through you. To ensure GFCI protection, use a GFCI circuit breaker in the panel or a GFCI receptacle. Regular receptacles can be GFCI protected if they are wired through the GFCI receptacle.

Special Systems

The kitchen is sometimes described as the nerve center of the modern home. Indeed, as cooking and cleaning become simpler, the kitchen is given over more to entertainment, communication, and home-management duties. Take advantage of the fact that you're opening the walls for electrical work to run hidden wires for these systems.

Telephone

Since deregulation, the telephone wall jacks and interior cables are owned by you, the subscriber. You may extend the lines from one jack to wherever another jack is needed. The components are modular, inexpensive, and available at any telephone-supply or home-electronics store. The extremely low voltage is not dangerous to work with, unless you have a pacemaker. Don't forget jacks for the computer modem and fax, which you will probably need eventually.

Doorbell

You may wish to add a chime unit in the kitchen so you can hear the front door better, add a push button at an exterior kitchen door, or install an entirely independent system for the kitchen. The doorbell transformer, on a junction box, steps down the house current to 10 to 20 volts. The wiring is low-voltage 16, 18, or 20 gauge.

Television Cable

Check with your cable supplier to be sure you are allowed to add additional cable outlets. In the wall where the cable enters your home, you can install a splitter, and then run a second cable through the wall to the kitchen. If this weakens the signal, you can install a small booster, or amplifier. All of these inexpensive, modular components are available from a home-electronics store.

Stereo Speakers

Bring music to the kitchen by running 12- or 14-gauge double wire, called lamp cord or zip-cord, from the stereo through the walls and ceiling to the desired location in the kitchen. Construct recesses in the walls, soffit boxes, or special cubby-holes in the cabinets to house the speakers and wire.

Smoke Detectors

Hard-wired smoke detectors are required by some codes, especially in rental units. They can be wired so that when one alarm is activated, they all sound—a wonderful advantage if the kitchen and bedrooms are far apart. This requires that they all be on a single circuit, wired with a three-conductor cable. A photoelectric alarm is best for the kitchen; ionization alarms are easily tripped by normal cooking fumes.

Surge Suppressor

If you will have a computer in the kitchen, a built-in surge suppressor eliminates the need for a modular one. The surge-suppressor receptacle is installed in an electrical box like a regular 120-volt receptacle.

Remember electrical needs on kitchen islands. A strip of receptacles provides juice for a multitude of modern appliances on this cantilevered work surface.

IGHTING

Well-planned lighting in the kitchen is a matter of efficiency and safety, as well as good looks. Fixtures must be positioned both for soft ambient light and for useful task light. Switches should provide convenient control from several locations and allow various combinations of lighting type and intensity.

Lighting Design

Although light is not tangible, it must be as carefully designed as every other element in a kitchen. Even the most elegant kitchen is ultimately a workroom, and must be lighted with utility in mind.

Throughout the day, the kitchen lighting needs will vary: perhaps none at all on a sunny day, to full lighting for evening dinner preparation and socializing, to a dim nightlight for the midnight snacker. Every kitchen needs both general and task lighting, as well as lighting at a certain minimum level.

Within these guidelines there is wide leeway for expressing your personal style. Do you feel cheeriest in a kitchen bathed in cool, white, shadowless light? Or do you prefer focused light that entertains your eye with varied levels of intensity? Do you wish to emphasize the sleek, smooth surfaces of a modern kitchen, or to bring out the dramatic textures of rustic wood and tile? Would a piece of neon art add light and drama to your kitchen? You can design lighting to fit any of these preferences while providing a safe and efficient workplace.

While deciding on your needs in general and task lighting, consider how the two will work together for optimum convenience and variety.

General Lighting

General lighting illuminates the space as a whole, eliminating dangerous shadowed areas, and allowing you to see into cabinets and drawers. This may be accomplished with ceiling fixtures, fluorescent panels, pendant lighting, or downlighting, either recessed or on tracks.

Energy codes for new construction or remodeling require the dominant lighting to be fluorescent fixtures. Dominant

Along with filling general and specific task needs, lighting can also achieve special effects in the nighttime kitchen. Lighting from long incandescent tubes in the soffit space gives this kitchen ceiling a moonlit glow.

refers to the light turned on with the switch at the entrance to the room. Existing fixtures can be refitted with fluorescent bulbs or replaced with up-to-date fixtures that incorporate the use of fluorescence.

Experts differ on how much general light a kitchen should have. Needs determine this to a large extent. Contemplate your taste in lighting, remembering the visual needs of family members (older people need more light). Speculate on the future activity level of the new kitchen, because multiple uses require extra light.

The colors you use in the kitchen affect whether light is reflected or absorbed: Light-colored cabinets and countertops require less lighting than dark wood tones. A kitchen with a ceiling higher than 8 feet requires more general light; a kitchen with a lot of task lighting may require less. With these variables in mind, consider the following figures as minimums in establishing a general-lighting level.

Incandescent
80 square feet—200 watts
150 square feet—300 watts
250 square feet—500 watts

Fluorescent
80 square feet—150 watts
150 square feet—220 watts
250 square feet—350 watts

Task Lighting

Task lighting must be carefully planned for direct illumination of the kitchen work centers—food preparation, cleanup, and home office. It also fills in the dark nooks and crannies on countertops created by overhanging wall cabinets. For the latter, nothing beats fluorescent tubes, surface-mounted on the underside of the cabinets. A tube should be two-thirds the length of the counter it lights and provide about 8 watts of power per foot of counter. For example, a 6-foot run of counter calls for a 4-foot fluorescent tube of about 48 watts—a 40-watt tube would suffice. The tube should be mounted close to the front edge of the cabinets. It can be concealed by adding a valance—a matching strip of wood or laminate—to the bottom edge of the cabinet. In a traditional kitchen, a stained-glass valance provides a beautiful effect when lighted. To enhance a high-tech style, mini track lights can also be mounted under cabinets; no valance is necessary.

The conventional choices for illuminating work centers, including islands, are recessed downlights, track lights, or pendant lights. Keep in mind that none of these will fully light a countertop beneath a wall cabinet. Each work center should be lighted with a minimum of 100 to 150 watts of incandescent light or 40 to 60 watts of fluorescent light—more if you prefer it bright.

Fixture Types

All permanent fixtures are wired into the electrical circuit at an electrical box. You must plan the location of your fixtures in advance so that the boxes can be installed when the wiring is done. Kitchen lights must be on their own 15-amp or 20-amp circuit, not part of any appliance or receptacle circuit.

Consider combining several types of lighting within your kitchen. Here, tracks illuminate the work centers while small recessed lights spotlight items on the display shelves.

Panels

Fluorescent panel fixtures are the most common means of producing general light in the kitchen. Tubes are housed in rectangular box fixtures. Individual fixtures may be recessed into the ceiling between joists or surface-mounted on the ceiling, although this is less attractive. Several fixtures may be surface-mounted and covered by a suspended ceiling—translucent panels in a metal or wood frame—which diffuses the light.

A variation of this is the dome-light ceiling, in which fluorescent fixtures are mounted around the ceiling perimeter and the translucent panels fitted between the ceiling and wall, often forming an angled soffit over wall cabinets. This is a practical style for ceilings that are only 8 feet high and allows another fixture to be mounted in the center of the ceiling. All panels bathe the room in a cool, even glow, but dome lights may be more strictly directed and still illuminate the room.

Pendants

Also called hanging lights, pendants achieve both general- and task-lighting needs. As an accent install a pendant low over a table or bar. For general lighting the fixture should cast diffused light downward, outward, and upward toward the ceiling, where it will bounce back down into the room. A heavy fixture, such as a light with a ceiling fan, needs to be supported by screwing the box into a stud, and sometimes affixing a horizontal metal mounting strap as well.

Recessed

For task lighting, nothing beats a recessed light, aimed at a specific work center. Plan the cones of light to overlap, adding to the ambient light. Recessed fixtures include canister-shaped downlights, as well as fluorescent fixtures, which are usually in the form of a metal box. Recessed light can be installed in the ceiling or in an overhanging soffit box. Install lights upward from cabinet tops to wash the ceiling with a glossy, white general light. Make sure there is enough vertical clearance to accept these fixtures. They need space around them to dissipate heat.

Tracks

Track lights enable several fixtures to run from one electrical box. Tracks are fitted to mounting clips attached to the ceiling or attached to it directly. Some tracks are designed to be wired into two different circuits for greater lighting flexibility.

Accents

Use the soffit space or picture-rail molding to encase strands of Tivoli bulbs, like Christmas tree lights, or neon strips for creative designs.

Switches

Each entrance to the kitchen should have switches that control the primary general and task lights. Switches are usually located 44 to 48 inches above the floor—you may locate them differently for special needs or to accommodate your design. If the kitchen has two or more entrances, use three-way switches. Any special-purpose task light that you wish to operate independently, such as a grow light for plants or a light over a bar, should have its own switch on the wall nearest it.

One convenient switching arrangement is to wire the task lights to one switch and the general lights to another, so that you can use one or the other or both at once. Another method is to wire the fluorescent lights and the incandescent lights to separate switches, to allow for different temperatures and lighting moods. Dimmers must be installed on separate switches. You may also want to put a pendant light over the dining table on a separate switch.

A light switch requires an electrical box, the same as fixtures and receptacles. At each kitchen entrance, you may combine the electrical boxes for two or even three or more switches—these are called gang boxes. Several different styles of switches provide fine control over lighting.

• A single-pole switch, the typical on-off switch, offers control from only one location, making it suitable for a kitchen with only one entrance.

• Three-way switches work in pairs. One is placed at each of two entrances, enabling you to turn lights on at one entrance and off at the other. They are a must if your kitchen has an exterior door or if you are able to walk through the kitchen from one room to another.

• A dimmer switch allows you to adjust the intensity of the light to your mood and needs. The switch uses a rheostat to reduce the flow of current. The most economical is a rotary or sliding dimmer, which requires that you dim the light all the way to reach the *off* position; gradually extinguishing a light this way increases the life of the bulb and saves energy. Dimmers are available for fluorescent lights, but they are expensive and require a special fixture in limited styles. A simple alternative is to wire fluorescent fixtures on two different switches.

• Specialty switches range from practical to fun. A mercury switch uses a rolling drop of liquid mercury to turn on and off smoothly and absolutely silently. A time-clock switch has a dial that can be set to turn the lights on and off at preset times. A lighted switch has a toggle that glows in the dark so it's easy to locate. A clock switch has a tiny digital time display built-in.

HEATING AND COOLING

When planning kitchen heating, keep in mind that the range, refrigerator, dishwasher, and clothes dryer all do their part to keep the room warm, especially if it's well insulated. Cooling the kitchen will be requisite, and may be as simple as ensuring proper ventilation and installing sunshades on the windows.

System Solutions

In most kitchen remodeling, the existing heating and cooling systems are kept intact, and require only small modifications to fit the new floor plan. In a central forced-air system, this might entail extending an air duct to reposition the vent. If your ducts run under the floor or over the ceiling, as most do, this is fairly simple, but in some systems a change may require opening the wall or ceiling. The ducting may be rectangular sheet metal, or a flexible insulated tubing. A convenient vent position is in the toe kick of the cabinets; this is basically a floor vent with a 90-degree adapter sleeve called a transition elbow. The sink toe kick is often recommended as a location, but you might be bothered by the blast of hot air on your feet as you do the dishes. Locate a vent to direct heating or cooling to where it's most needed: a breakfast nook surrounded by windows, for example.

To save work and expense, make an effort to extend the existing ducts as simply as possible. If the new kitchen will add square footage to the house, check whether the existing furnace and air conditioner can handle the extra load. Rather than upgrading the system, you might prefer to install supplemental heating or cooling in the new kitchen. Some options include a 240-volt baseboard heater, or a window air conditioner/heat pump—each requires its own electrical circuit. These are simple, efficient solutions for a space that was never tied into the central heating system of the house.

If the house has a hot-water heating system, replace any radiators in the kitchen with baseboard convectors to gain space and increase design options. Most heating pipes are galvanized steel, but new pipes may be copper, unless local codes prohibit this. Moving or extending the heating pipes is a straightforward plumbing task, complicated, of course, if you need to enter the walls for access. Shift any exposed pipes into the walls, or construct a box, called a chase, around them if this can be done unobtrusively.

For the ultimate luxury in hot-water heating, look into installing an under-floor radiant heating system. Pipes beneath the subfloor warm the floor, which gently radiates heat upward. This is a lovely feeling, especially for a ceramic-tile floor in winter. It also circumvents the lack of kitchen wall space for heating units.

Nonsystem Solutions

Naturally, heating and cooling do not have to be mechanical. Well-placed windows can moderate the temperature through much of the year by providing cross-ventilation. Sunshine, especially through a skylight, will warm the kitchen dramatically. In summer, this effect can be minimized by using blinds or installing a sunshade on the skylight. Install awnings to shield windows from the sun, and interior shutters, especially if they are lined and padded, to insulate from the cold.

A wood-burning stove can provide the main source of heat for the kitchen; of course, it will also make itself the focal point of your kitchen design. The stove must have at least 36 inches of clearance from the wall, and may require heat shielding on the walls and floor. It has an insulated chimney pipe that extends out through the roof. The local building code has installation requirements. A prefabricated fireplace insert with glass doors and a venting system can also be counted on for heating, but a conventional fireplace may rob more heat than it creates, depending on its construction.

A ceiling fan with a reversible motor draws cool air upward in summer and circulates warm air downward in winter.

Insulation has a great impact on energy efficiency and should be upgraded during remodeling. All exterior walls must be insulated. Any work that requires opening an exterior wall provides an opportunity to replace the insulation if necessary.

Plan heating vents away from warmth-generating appliances, such as ovens, cooktops, and dishwashers, and near areas where the heat will be welcomed. A practical heating-vent placement, as in this kitchen, is in the toe kick near the eating area.

ITALY

CHOOSING CABINETS, FIXTURES, AND APPLIANCES

The degree to which the new kitchen suits your needs depends largely on how well you put together the fixtures and appliances. As with the construction elements, there is a range of type and quality of fixtures and appliances to meet every budget. Kitchen fixtures include cabinets and the myriad fittings within them, countertops, and sinks and faucets. Major kitchen appliances are the large appliances—the dishwasher, cooking appliances, refrigerator, and freezer. Less glamorous—but equally necessary—are the garbage, recycling, and ventilating systems included in a well-designed kitchen.

Base your choices for cabinets, fixtures, and appliances on how each suits your kitchen style and theme, the measurements of the preliminary floor plan, your maintenance requirements, and your budget. The traditional country charm of this kitchen, also pictured on page 1, is enhanced by open shelves, which display collections and cooking items.

CABINETS

Think of cabinets as furniture for the kitchen. They should be a pleasure to look at and comfortable to live with. More than any other fixture, the cabinets will express the style of your kitchen. Their locations and features will also determine whether the kitchen is an organized and convenient place to work.

Choosing Cabinets

There are several different sources for new cabinets. You can buy them from stock, order custom modular units, or have cabinets built to order. The type of manufacturer you choose will determine the price range, type of construction, waiting period, and amount of customizing available. Use the following procedure for choosing new cabinets.

- Evaluate your storage needs.
- Assess the amount of storage capacity desired.
- Measure the space available for different storage areas.
- Decide on the type and quality of cabinets that you can afford.
- Pick the exterior style and finish of cabinets.
- Choose the interior features you need.
- Select the hardware that will work best for you, the cabinet type, and the kitchen look.

As you shop, you will come across various design terms from different manufacturers. What is significant in choosing cabinets is not the name of the design but how it fits your kitchen.

Stock Cabinets

Also called ready-made, knockdown, or ready-to-assemble, stock cabinets are made in large factories on an assembly line. The units are shipped in cartons and put together on site; some are totally unassembled and packed flat. They come in standard sizes and shapes to suit most basic kitchens. While no custom orders are taken, you can choose from a large range of styles and materials. Stock cabinets have a short order period and are sometimes

Use the principles of design to coordinate elements in every price range. Although the materials in this kitchen are not the most expensive, the design is appealing because of the manner in which they have been combined. The black edges of these refaced cabinets match the accents of the resilient flooring. For added visual rhythm the doors to the dining room and pass-through (behind the flowers in the background) have been painted black and white.

available immediately. They are your least expensive option and can offer quite a bit of style for the money. The price and quality of cabinets vary widely; pay close attention to the following construction details.

- Are joints both glued and screwed, or connected with other secure special-purpose fasteners?
- Is the wood grain well matched? Are the edges clean and smooth?
- Is the surface laminate durable and of high quality?
- Is the core material of adequate strength for your needs?
- Are the interiors finished neatly?
- Are doors and drawers straight and even? Are cabinet frames square?
- Is the hardware strong and skillfully installed?
- Are shelf supports adequate?
- How much assembly will be necessary?

Custom Modular Cabinets

Also called special-order cabinets, custom modular cabinets are factory-made to your specifications. You choose the type of wood or laminate surface, the door and hardware styles, and the cabinet sizes and configurations from the standard range offered by the manufacturer, and your set of cabinets is built to order.

The advantages are that you get exactly the combination of features you want and, since the cabinets are all built at once, possible variations in wood grain, finish, or laminate color are controlled. You can special order custom cabinets in odd sizes or equipped with features not found in stock lines.

The large factories that make these cabinets have sophisticated joining equipment, and their finish application is generally superior to that of smaller shops. Both the quality and price of custom modular cabinets tend to be higher than for stock cabinets, but they vary widely. Order time is longer; it can range from 5 to 15 weeks.

Built-to-Order Cabinets

Also called custom-made cabinets, these are the ne plus ultra of kitchen fittings. Like fine custom furniture, these cabinets are individually built of the finest materials to your exact specifications—no modular sizes or standard materials inhibit your desires. Many built-to-order cabinets are fashioned of fine hardwood, or they may have a unique design or finish available no other way. The cabinets may be extended to include a coordinated dining buffet, wine bar, or stereo center in an adjoining room. These cabinets may be imported, domestic, or made by a local shop. The fabricator's representative—or the cabinetmaker—will come to your home to measure the kitchen and will work closely with you during the design process. The advantage is that you end up with one-of-a-kind kitchen furnishings perfectly suited to your needs and style. Of course, all this perfection comes at a price. An economical alternative to a built-to-order kitchen is to install custom modular cabinets, and have a particular showpiece or unique functional item built to order. Depending on the size of the job, its materials, and the order backlog, fabrication time can be many months.

Specifying built-to-order cabinets allows flexibility in your floor plan and gives you freedom of choice in styling the room to your heart's desire. A traditional kitchen with a Roman theme is achieved here by heavily detailed wood cabinets and solid-surface-material countertops made to look like natural marble.

Cabinet Construction

The construction of a cabinet entails more than meets the eye. Along with deciding on a look that fits your kitchen, you must select the type of frame, door style, construction material, interior design, and hardware.

Frames

Despite the countless styles available, there are only two types of cabinet construction: frame and frameless. In frame construction, the body of the cabinet is formed by a wood skeleton enclosing thin wood panels; the doors are usually frame-and-panel too. The frame provides rigidity and support for the cabinet and its contents. Frame construction is a traditional cabinetmakers' art and lends a note of grace to any cabinet style. A common variation is face-frame construction, in which only the front of the cabinet has a frame, and the sides, top, bottom, and back are assembled with dado joints.

Frameless construction, sometimes called European style, is a newer technique in which the sides, top, bottom, and back of the cabinet are joined with special fasteners to form a box. The doors completely cover the front of the box. This makes a smooth, clean-lined design that lends itself to modern styles and the use of laminate surfaces.

Doors

The way a door or drawer face is fitted to the cabinet determines to a great degree the overall look of the cabinet. There are three basic door fittings: overlaid, flush, and partially inset.

Frameless cabinets always have an overlaid door, in which the entire door panel rests against the front of the cabinet. The hinges are hidden, and rows of doors form an almost seamless, smooth facade—a very sleek and modern look. On frame cabinets, overlaid doors will usually show the outline of the face frame, a somewhat rustic, boxy look.

Flush doors fit entirely inside the face frame when closed, forming a flat surface that reveals the frame and hides the door edges. This can provide a smooth, simple facade, but often the hinges are partially exposed.

Partially inset doors have a lip along their edges that overlaps the face frame, although the main body of the door fits within the frame. The door appears to overlay the frame, but in a slimmer, lighter way.

All three styles can be equally sturdy and efficient; how well they perform is dependent on the quality of the hardware. All three types are available in designs to fit almost any kitchen. Overlaid doors are generally modern, flush doors may be modern or traditional, and partially inset doors come in the widest range of modern and traditional designs.

Door Fronts

All door styles are available with different designs on the front face to fit different looks.

For a modern kitchen, choose a door with a smooth, flat-front panel, with either veneer or laminate surfaces, perhaps with continuous wood or metal pulls across the tops or with wood or metal edging on a least two edges.

Wood cabinets bring a natural warmth to every style of kitchen. Here a glass-panel door within a run of cabinets and the inlay of contrasting wood below the countertop edge add interest to the beautiful wood cabinets.

For a traditional look, choose a door with dimension—horizontal rails and vertical stiles around an inset panel that is raised, flush, or recessed. The panel may be solid wood, veneered plywood, or glass. Its top can be arched or square. The top rail above the panel might be carved or stenciled.

Materials and Finishes

Along with the strength of the joints and hardware, the overall quality of the cabinet is a combination of the grade and thickness of the core and surface materials.

Core Material

The cabinet core material will usually be particleboard, plywood, or metal. Particleboard is stiff, smooth, warp resistant, and very heavy. It is made in many different grades for different applications; a board rated 45-pound commercial grade is excellent for cabinets.

Plywood makes a stronger, more warp-resistant cabinet than solid lumber does. First-rate cabinets use a high-quality, solid-core plywood with a knot-free surface. The ultimate is a furniture-grade solid-hardwood plywood with a fine hardwood veneer. Check the inside and back of the cabinet when investigating the quality of materials.

Metal cabinets are recommended mainly for families with special needs, such as construction-material allergies, or to attain a unique look.

For a frame cabinet, the minimum thickness of wood-based core material should be ½ inch; for a frameless cabinet, ⅝ to ¾ inch is recommended.

Laminate

Although usually a very thin layer, the surface material is what gives a cabinet its feel, its sense of weight, and a large degree of its style. It must also be durable enough to withstand daily bumps, scratches, and scrubbing.

Laminates, referred to by designers as mica, have a smooth, seamless surface that lends itself to modern, clean-lined cabinet design. They are manufactured in several performance levels. Pay attention to prices when shopping for laminate cabinets; those that are much cheaper than average probably have a less-durable laminate, but the trade-off may be worthwhile if the cabinets are well constructed.

High-pressure laminate (HPL) is the thickest, most durable and the most commonly used; it is also expensive. Because it can imitate natural wood grain, a lacquer finish, or even metal, the look of laminate is an attractive design statement on its own, and HPL boasts hundreds of colors and textures. The same high-pressure laminate can be used for both cabinets and countertops for a simple, unified, custom look.

Low-pressure laminate (LPL), also known as melamine, has a base of paper or polyester and usually comes heat-fused to a light substrate material. Although not so thick or durable as HPL, it is cheaper and may well meet your needs.

Economically between HPL and LPL is continuous high-performance laminate (CHPL), which is similar to HPL but is thinner and softer. While it performs almost as well as HPL, it is less expensive.

Wood

A well-made set of wood cabinets will have a coordinated grain pattern and color. The very best—and most expensive—will have a grain that continues unbroken across the line of cabinets or that is mirrored symmetrically in an effect called tabling or booking.

Hardwoods are usually used for kitchen-cabinets. For cabinets that will be left natural or stained, use oak—the most popular—maple, cherry, walnut, mahogany, teak, or pine.

For cabinets that will be painted, choose ash, beech, birch, or poplar, which are smooth and not highly grained.

When specifying a species of wood for your cabinets, be sure you know whether it is a color or a grain pattern you are after. For example, oak, a relatively cheap hardwood, can be given a walnut stain, satisfying your desire for walnut cabinets at a lower price.

Most wood cabinets are delivered prefinished. When buying stock cabinets, check that the color and level of gloss is consistent. When buying custom modular and built-to-order cabinets, request your preference of stain color and level of gloss in the clear finish.

How many pineapples can you find in this kitchen? The traditional Hawaiian symbol of welcome is pressed into tin door fronts and stenciled onto the floor and backsplash for a united design motif.

Interior Design

Most people complain now and then that their kitchen cabinets don't have enough space, but storage problems are often caused by the inefficient use of adequate cabinet space. When designing your cabinet locations, keep in mind that hard-to-reach storage space simply won't be used.

In general, drawers and rollouts of various widths and depths offer more accessible storage in base cabinets than do shelves. All shelves should be adjustable in height. Frameless cabinets have more accessible interior space—side to side—than frame cabinets, so these may be a sensible choice if cabinet space is tight.

Some of the most remarkable changes in kitchen design have been in the fittings inside cabinets. Spend time figuring your needs and look through cabinet catalogs and in showrooms for features that will increase the efficiency of your storage. Some of the novel fittings available for inside of cabinets include:

- Swing-out spice rack with shelves behind
- Revolving lazy susan for corner cabinets
- Pull-out towel bars
- Door-mounted racks
- Vertical tray dividers
- Roll-out trash and recycling bins

Hardware

A multitude of hinges, pulls, and glides, designed especially for kitchen cabinets, provides specialized function as well as style.

Visible hinges and pulls should coordinate with the look of the kitchen cabinets and may be a notable design highlight for the room. In general, a modern cabinet calls for hinges and pulls of simple design and material: a plain laminate cabinet with continuous brushed-aluminum pulls, for example, or a plastic or steel C-pull. A traditional cabinet calls for dressier hardware, such as a frame-and-panel cherry cabinet with visible bronze or brass hinges and a polished brass handle with a backplate. A period cabinet should have historically correct hardware. Black wrought-iron surface hinges and latches complement a Colonial-style cabinet.

Personalize cabinets inside and out. Decoratively painted cabinet doors (above) can be achieved through stencils or artistic talent. Space-saving interior hardware (below) is available for drawers, wall cabinets, and base cabinets.

Specialty Cabinets

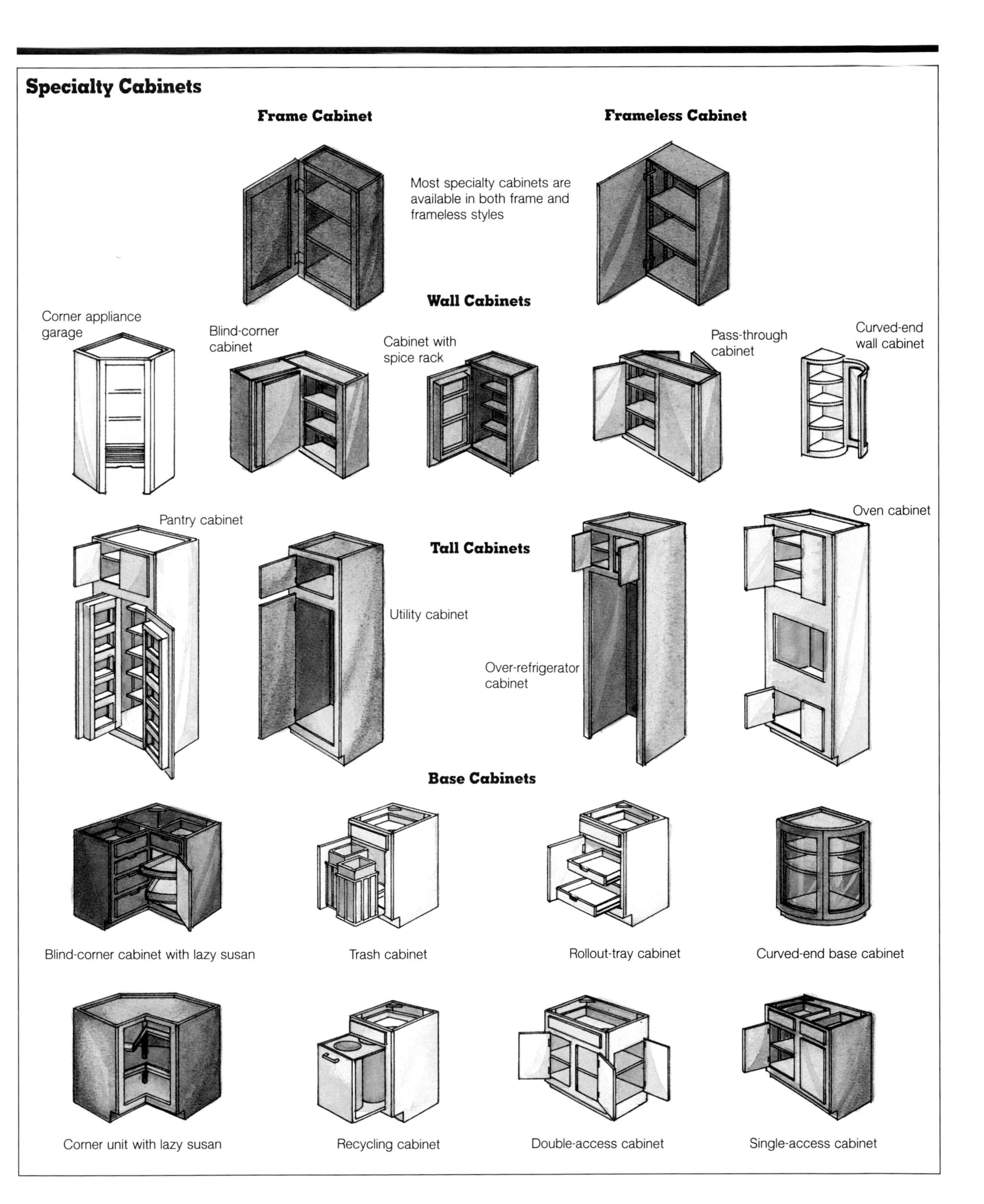

Hinges

A new cabinet-door hinge is a complex little machine that steadies the door when open, pulls the door snug against the cabinet when closed, and adjusts to straighten a sagging door. Hinges may be hidden, partly exposed, or surface-mounted, depending on the cabinet style. Hidden hinges are most often used in a modern style, where a smooth, unbroken surface is desired.

Check hinge quality carefully when cabinet shopping. Kitchen-cabinet doors take a lot of abuse.

Pulls

A pull may take the form of a knob or a handle, a finger notch recessed into the cabinet face, or a continuous wood or metal strip mounted on the top or bottom of the door. Its function is as much design as utility. When choosing a pull style, take into account the size of the smallest drawer and largest door and pick a pull that suits both in scale. Height and width of door and drawer rails, stiles, and panels—and ease of use—determine the horizontal and vertical placement of pulls.

Choose a pull color that blends with or contrasts the cabinet color or as an accent—to bring out a color used elsewhere in the kitchen.

Remember to include the protrusion of the pull when measuring cabinet clearances. Always try a pull before buying to be sure it fits your fingers (and fingernails!).

Glides

Totally hidden and absolutely vital to an effective storage system, glides support drawers and roll-out shelves, allowing them to slide effortlessly in and out without wear. A typical glide, mounted on the side or bottom of a drawer, has a metal track that moves along nylon rollers. A stop at the front of the track keeps the drawer or shelf from falling out; it can be depressed for removal.

Most frame cabinets have wood drawers with slides mounted on the side or bottom. Frameless cabinets have glides as an integral part of the drawer side. Some glides have an extension that allows a heavy drawer to be pulled out all the way. A small drawer may have simpler glides or none at all.

Check glide quality with the drawer carrying a full load, if possible. Also check the ease of removal and reinsertion. Note whether glides have rough metal edges or are smoothly coated so they won't cut your fingers.

Specialty Units

Cabinet manufacturers—and certainly cabinet craftspeople—produce specialty units for particular needs. New designs are introduced every year. Their appropriateness for your new kitchen is a matter of personal judgment; check your wish list to see how suitable these and other specialty units would be to you (see page 73).

Open display shelves coordinated with the cabinets give the kitchen a cohesive appearance and can be purchased to fit perfectly between units.

Appliance Garage

Because tambour doors, seen here on the island, behind the desk, and covering the corner appliance garage, provide interior access without having to allow for door swing, they are a good choice for tight spaces.

An appliance garage clears counters of the array of small appliances taken for granted in the modern kitchen. The garage usually consists of an oversized built-in cabinet covered by a tambour door, which rolls over the garage space and down to the countertop to hide small appliances, a television, or a microwave oven. If you plan an appliance garage, install appropriate electrical receptacles at the back of it so appliances can remain plugged in between uses. Make sure the height will accommodate your tallest appliance, the depth will accommodate your deepest, and the counter space remaining in front will be sufficient.

Pull-out Counters

A pull-out counter hidden behind a drawer front can be extended to provide extra counter space, a chopping block, or small table. Some styles sit on legs. Others pull away completely from the cabinet face or box and can be rolled around for portable use. These countertops are handy for discrete tasks, such as rolling out dough or using a food processor. They do not have to be installed at countertop height, and can be placed in the middle of the run of drawers for use by children or someone in a wheelchair.

Ironing Cabinets

Ironing board cabinets are available in several styles. Some pull out from behind a drawer front; others fold down from a wall or tall cabinet. Some contain only the board; others provide storage for clothing items, starch and supplies, and the iron itself. Remember that you need to plan an electrical receptacle near the ironing area and sufficient work space on one side of the board.

Find specialty units to satisfy kitchen activity desires. Appliance garages (above left), often recessed into otherwise unused wall space, keep small appliances handy yet hidden. Space-saving ironing board cabinets (above right) have resurged in popularity as home square footage declines. Desk units (below) made to match other kitchen cabinets are available from many manufacturers.

Specialized Drawers

Specialized food drawers are deeper than standard, lined with metal, and have sliding lids to keep bulk dry goods easily accessible. Some have a perforated bottom for ventilating root vegetables.

A sink-front bin is a hinged drawer front that opens to access a tray for sponges and scrubbers. This tilt-out, occupying a formerly wasted space, hides the most common, least-attractive sink accessories.

Desk units that match kitchen cabinets may contain file drawers and computer-component shelves. Cabinets above may have pigeonholes or drawers and shelves. Often covered by a tambour door, these units look and work like a rolltop desk.

Bar units can include bottle drawers and stemware racks. Plan plumbing for a bar sink and ice maker, and receptacles for a refrigerator to complete the party center.

Measuring for Cabinets

Cabinets are made in standard dimensions that comply with architectural design standards and appliance sizes. This enables you to assemble your cabinets building-block style. Most American-made cabinets increase in 3-inch width increments, starting as narrow as 9 inches to more than 60 inches. Some frameless and all European-made cabinets are based on the metric system. (See the metric conversion chart on page 112.) If you choose metric cabinets, carefully verify that appliances will fit with them.

Each manufacturer offers a specific range of cabinet sizes; not all styles may be available in all sizes. Ask for a specification sheet.

Base Cabinets

Standard base cabinets are 24 inches deep and 34½ inches high, including a 4- or 4½-inch toe kick. Some European styles have higher toe kicks. A conventional countertop substrate of 1½ inches brings the countertop height to 36 inches. You can customize the countertop height by building up or cutting down the toe kick; making the countertop substrate thicker; or adding a narrow plinth, filler strip, or row of shallow drawers along the top of the cabinets under the counter. Keep in mind that the standard range or dishwasher is made to fit a 36-inch-high countertop. Of course, custom cabinets can be made for specific needs.

Wall Cabinets

Typically, wall cabinets measure 12 to 13 inches deep and 12 to 36 inches high, although standard cabinets come as high as 42 or 48 inches. Custom units can be built for special uses. Widths range from as narrow as 9 inches to more than 48 inches. Even if you modify the height of the base cabinets, the wall cabinets should be set 15 to 18 inches above the countertop, 25 inches above an island or peninsula, and 27 to 30 inches over a cooktop. A 15-inch-tall cabinet fits over a standard refrigerator; an 18-inch cabinet goes over a hood/vent.

Tall Cabinets

Pantry and broom-closet cabinets are usually 84 inches high and 12 to 48 inches wide. Some manufacturers offer this cabinet at 96 inches high. Tall cabinets are also made to fit microwaves and single and double wall ovens. Remember that if you raise or lower the height of the wall cabinets, you must also modify the tall cabinet accordingly, so its top will line up.

If your wish list includes a pantry but your floor plan doesn't allow space for one, consider a tall pantry cabinet equipped with door shelves, which handles dry storage needs in a minimum of space.

Reusing Existing Fixtures

One way to keep your costs down is to retain and refinish the existing cabinets, fixtures, and appliances.

Cabinets

There are several options for using your existing cabinets, all of which will save you money compared to buying all-new ones. Also consider retaining the cabinet body and replacing only the doors. You may be able to buy several all-new cabinets with some matching doors for the existing cabinets. If the existing cabinets won't work in the new kitchen, keep them to use in the pantry, garage, laundry room, or other storage area.

Before deciding to retain existing cabinets, check their construction. Are they solid and well joined? Is their core material—whether hardwood, plywood, or particleboard—still in fair condition? Do the joints need reinforcement? Measure the cabinets to determine where they will fit in your new design.

Your refinishing alternatives depend on the cabinet material. Fine hardwood, hardwood veneer, or pine cabinets meant for a natural finish can be stripped of varnish; dark-stained wood can be bleached lighter. The wood can then be revarnished with a semigloss polyurethane, or oiled, or pickled with a pastel wash that allows the grain to show through. If the cabinets have inset-panel doors, the panels can be replaced with clear- or stained-glass panes, pierced tin, or even shirred fabric. On plain, flat doors, the addition of decorative molding provides a provincial detail. A flat band of wood applied as a frame around the door edges gives the illusion of a panel door. Metal and paint-quality wood cabinets can be stripped and repainted.

The easiest way to change the look of your cabinets is to install new hardware. Different knobs, pulls, and hinges may be all the refurbishing your cabinets require.

Countertops

Most countertops consist of a sturdy substrate, usually plywood, tile-backing board, or particleboard, sheathed with a surfacing material, commonly laminate, ceramic tile, or butcher-block wood. If you plan to leave the counter in place, you can resurface the countertop, but if you plan to replace the base cabinets, there is little reason to save and refinish the countertop. Be sure the substrate is sound before considering refinishing rather than replacing a countertop.

Cover a laminate countertop with either a new laminate, a stone slab, or ceramic or stone tile. Ceramic tile will last for decades. If you like the look of the existing tile and the original installation is still intact, you can simply clean and regrout the tiles. Tile can be reglazed a new color by a professional using spray equipment. The disadvantage of this is that the grout ends up the same color as the tile. Wood countertops can be sanded and oiled or covered by laminate or stone slab.

Sinks

Whether or not you plan to relocate the sink, you can retain the existing fixture so long as it is structurally sound. If you are satisfied with the size and configuration of the existing sink, by all means dismount, refurbish, and reuse it. The most common problems are chips, worn spots, and stains in the porcelain or enamel coating. Stainless steel sinks are virtually indestructible, although they may sustain dents or scratches, or the surface can develop rust stains or water spots. You can buff a stainless steel sink with special cleaning compound to restore the surface. Porcelain and enamel sinks can be professionally touched up, or refinished in a new color to match the new kitchen.

If you plan to install a new sink, save money by using the old one in the laundry room, gardening area, or bar as a utility sink. If you decide to retain and spruce up your old sink, remember that a new faucet or other fixture must fit the existing accessory holes.

Cooking Appliances

The expected life span of a range, cooktop, or oven is 15 years. If you are satisfied with your existing appliances, there is no need to discard them simply because the finish is worn or you don't like the color. Cooking appliances can be refinished by a professional porcelain/enamel repairer. Chips in porcelain can be filled with a durable resin that matches the original color, or the entire appliance can be re-enameled in any color you choose. This is especially rewarding if you wish to restore a vintage range.

Chrome replacement parts for newer appliances can be ordered from the manufacturer, or parts can be rechromed at an auto-body shop. Having a range painted at an auto-body shop is not recommended because automobile-exterior paints are not healthy for use inside the home.

If you like your current range, but also like the idea of a component cooking system, plan to keep the range and add other cooking appliances to the kitchen. If your range is electric, consider adding a gas cooktop, which would be especially convenient if the electric power went out.

Refrigerators

If your refrigerator and freezer are sound and fulfill your cold-storage needs, include these appliances in the new design. If you hope to purchase a larger unit in the future, allow space for it when planning the new kitchen.

It is possible to refinish refrigerators and freezers. They can be painted, and doors can be fitted with panels that match cabinets.

If the appliances no longer work well, be sure to dispose of them properly.

COUNTERTOPS

Because a typical kitchen countertop must withstand a range of abuses from vegetable chopping to plant potting yet remain smooth and sanitary with the wipe of a sponge, different work centers may call for unique surfaces. Consider the alternatives, then tailor each countertop to its specific purposes.

Choosing Countertops

There are several ways to purchase countertops, depending on the material and your budget. Some laminates are available prefabricated in standard sizes; however, most countertops are built to spec.

When choosing new countertops, be sure to cover all of the following points.

- Choose the type of sink.
- Calculate the square footage of countertop surface.
- Decide on the best material for each work center.
- Consider the maintenance of various materials.
- Figure in backsplash and edge-treatment designs.
- Determine the materials you can afford.

Materials

All the countertops in the kitchen can be made from the same material, which gives the room a cohesive look, or the countertop material can vary depending on its intended use. Reconcile multiple materials with coordinated backsplash and edge treatments.

When choosing the right countertop material, keep in mind initial costs, ease of maintenance, and life span of the material, as well as how it suits the look of the kitchen.

Laminates

Basically a plastic material, laminates for countertops are made in several grades. Only one type, high-pressure laminate (HPL), is durable enough to stand up to the punishments borne by kitchen countertops. This sandwich of paper layers, saturated with resins, and fused under heat and pressure, forms a sheet .05-inch thick—less than $^1/_{16}$ inch. (Some laminates are thinner, but grades less than .04-inch thick are not suitable for countertops.) Waterproof and easy to keep clean, HPL is ideal as a general countertop material. It comes in a seemingly limitless range of colors, textures, and patterns, and can be matched to laminate cabinets. Older-style laminates have a dark-colored core, which can be unsightly at edges; newer-style laminates, however, carry the surface color through the entire sheet.

Laminate is easy to cut and install, even on curves, and can be heat-formed on site. Its resistance to stains and wear is excellent, but knives scratch it, so it should not be used as a cutting surface. Laminate is much less expensive than stone, butcher block, and solid-surface material and is somewhat cheaper than ceramic tile.

Laminate can be purchased in sheets, usually 4 by 8 feet, to cut on site; or you can order custom sizes from a factory or supplier. Laminate can also be preinstalled on a substrate to be set onto the base cabinets. Such countertops are sold in standard sizes or can be special-ordered to fit your kitchen, and usually have an integral backsplash and front edge over which the laminate is curved to shape using heat, a process called post-forming. If you are special-ordering, let the dealer take the measurements, including sink and cooktop cutouts, preferably after the base cabinets have been installed, although a skilled individual can work from precise counter specs and room dimensions.

Ceramic and Dimensioned-Stone Tile

Available in thousands of colors, textures, and sizes, ceramic tile has a chameleon-like ability to blend with any kitchen style while making its own strong statement. Newly popular as a

This kitchen features refaced cabinets. The matching laminate countertop and cabinet surfaces present a unified look, and the contrasting drawer pulls keep the white from becoming overwhelming. A clever illusion, the mirrored soffit area makes the ceiling seem higher.

design element, tile has traditionally been prized in the kitchen for its durability, resistance to moisture and heat, and sanitary, easy-care surface. Installing tile is simple but requires patience and careful preparation. Although more costly than laminate, tile is less expensive than any other high-quality countertop material.

Thin cuts from natural marble, granite, or slate are called dimensioned-stone tiles. They provide a rich surface that is fairly stain resistant and can be used as a cutting surface. The tiles are usually 12 inches square and are installed in a manner similar to ceramic tile except that the grout joints are narrower. Stone tiles generally cost more than ceramic tiles but are less expensive than a slab countertop. Choose stone tiles ⅜- or ½-inch thick and be sure to check the color variety and graining of the natural product, as each piece is unique.

Both types of tile countertop have four main elements: the substrate, or base; the adhesive; the tiles; and the grout.

When buying ceramic tile, choose a high-fired tile, ½-inch thick, with a shiny or matte glaze finish. A vitreous or semivitreous tile has the necessary water resistance. Ask the tile dealer to direct you to those tiles specifically recommended for countertop use. Tiles with a raised pattern or a painted design will not wear well, but can be used as trim. The size and shape of the tile you choose will be integral to your kitchen design, but square tiles 4½ by 4½ inches or 6 by 6 inches are easiest to install, and fit the scale of most kitchens. Smaller tiles, called mosaics, measure 1 by 1 inch or 2 by 2 inches, and come pre-positioned on mesh-backed sheets that are 1 foot square. They are very durable.

Ceramic-tile countertops require a trim treatment on edges, along the backsplash, and around the openings for such fixtures as a sink or cooktop. When choosing tile, make sure that all the matching trim tiles you'll need are available. A tile countertop can also be edged with a strip of hardwood. The wood is screwed to the substrate and well sealed against moisture before the tile is layed.

When purchasing any type of tile, order at one time all the product needed, and check that any shade variations are not too extreme, although tiles always vary slightly. To figure the quantity, divide the total countertop area by the single-tile area, then add 5 percent for waste and repairs. Purchase trim tiles based on linear measurement.

Grout is a cement that fills the space between tiles. As part of the countertop surface, it must be durable and attractive. The grout joint should look proportional to the tile size and style; a wider joint gives a rustic look, and a narrower joint a sleek look. The joints will form a pronounced geometric pattern; consider whether this would clash with other patterns in the kitchen flooring, wallcovering, or fabrics. You can downplay the joints by choosing a colored grout that matches the tile. Many shades are available, and the dealer will have samples.

Install one type of countertop treatment throughout the room, such as the beautiful ceramic tile (above), for a traditional style, or combine various materials, like solid-surface-material sink treatment and a dimensioned-stone tile island (below), for a modern look.

Stone Slab

Earthy, luxurious stone presents a rich look when used on kitchen countertops. The stone types commonly used are marble, granite, and slate. Stone-slab countertops fit any kitchen style, adapting to both traditional and modern designs. However, the sheer weight and size can overpower a small space, and slabs are quite expensive. Consider using stone slabs for one countertop and coordinating other materials to it. Because stone slab is stain resistant, perfect for rolling dough, suitable as a cutting surface, and easy to clean, it's a stunning counterpart to butcher block.

Marble is a traditional countertop material, especially useful to bakers because of its cool, smooth surface. It comes in several colors and natural vein patterns, though white is most common for utilitarian kitchen use. Despite its seeming hardness, however, marble is porous and fairly soft, and it stains and scratches easily. A marble countertop can be fragile and difficult to maintain; it must be coated frequently with a penetrating sealer. Though an entire countertop can be made from a single marble slab, a recommended use for marble in the kitchen is as a countertop insert in the baking center. So-called cultured marble, made of marble chips and dust in an acrylic base, is not durable enough for kitchens.

Granite is growing increasingly popular as a countertop material. Harder than marble and far less porous, granite doesn't stain. It can be used like marble for baking and candy making, and hot pans will not damage it. Granite has a confetti-like variegated grain in any combination of white, black, gray, pink, and sometimes other colors. For a countertop, the surface should be highly polished. A 1¼-inch granite slab is strong enough to form a 12-inch overhang without needing extra support.

Slate also makes a durable and dramatic countertop if you wish to make a strong design statement. Although always dark in color, slate comes in shades of black, brown, green, blue, and gray. Slate absorbs heat and can become hot to the touch. Its rugged surface cannot take a high polish.

All stone-slab countertops are cut to order and finished by the dealer. Because of its great weight, a stone-slab countertop may require extra support bracing in the base cabinets—ask the cabinet dealer. Slabs typically come in thicknesses of ¾ inch or 1¼ inches; there is a considerable difference in weight, although not in cost. To make a thin countertop look more substantial, an extra strip can be glued along the bottom of the front edge. Stone-slab countertops are an expensive investment and should be installed by an expert.

Horizontal lines rather than the type of materials used are the hallmark of the modern-style kitchen. Natural granite countertops and backsplashes (above) fit the bill as perfectly as ones made of manufactured solid-surface material (below).

Solid-Surface Material

Known by brand names, such as Avonite® and Corian®, solid-surface material (SSM) was invented as a substitute for stone, but its practicality, beauty, and versatility have put it in a class by itself. A dense slab of polyester or acrylic, SSM is nonporous, waterproof, resistant to chemicals, and does not stain. Because the color and material go all the way through, little scratches and minor burns can be sanded out; although hot pans will cause damage. Its unusual properties give SSM unique design potential; it can be cut and routed, or heated and bent, to any custom shape. Where two pieces are joined, the seam is almost invisible. Liquid plastics can be applied to form intricate "inlayed" patterns in contrasting colors. Unlike laminates, SSM is waterproof at the edges and can be used around undermounted sinks. It can also be cast in one piece with an integral sink, a sleek look that is also easy to keep clean.

Countertops and backsplashes provide ample opportunity for self-expression. Ceramic-tile murals (above) bring seventeenth-century charm to a twentieth-century room, and an expansive butcher-block island countertop (below) provides a space for budding artists to create while dinner cooks.

Solid-surface material comes in thicknesses of ½ inch and ¾ inch. Either can be used for a countertop; an edge band of like material can be applied to make it look thicker. It is manufactured in a wide variety of faux-stone finishes and colors. Depending on your kitchen design, the fabricator may have to complete the installation on site. Some manufacturers require that a certified fabricator both measure and install their product before honoring the warranty. SSM is more expensive than laminate or tile, but less than stone slab. When considering an SSM countertop, be sure to include the cost of installation.

Wood

Warm and natural, wood makes for a quiet and forgiving countertop. Because of its soft and porous surface, wood requires more diligent upkeep than most countertops and it should not be used around sinks. Even a small area of wood countertop, such as an island or a cutting-board inset, will warm up the kitchen decor. Butcher block is the wood surface most often seen in the kitchen, because it makes a durable cutting surface that won't dull knives. It consists of narrow strips of maple, oak, or ash, or small blocks of wood set end-grain up, which are laminated together. It is available in a 25-inch width for countertops, and is usually 1½ inches thick. The edges can be cut or routed to suit the line of your kitchen. If you intend to prepare food on butcher block, finish it only with mineral oil or other food-grade oil.

Other types of wood make attractive countertops, although they should not be used for a cutting board. Materials to consider include high-quality, ¾-inch hardwood-veneer plywood, hardwood planks glued side by side, and even tongue-and-groove hardwood flooring over plywood. These must be handcrafted and will make your kitchen one of a kind. If you enjoy woodworking, you can design and make these yourself; otherwise, have them custom-made by a professional.

Backsplashes

A backsplash protects the wall above the countertop from heat, water, and spills. It may be 4 or 5 inches high or extend all the way up to the wall cabinets. The backsplash is often an integral part of the countertop and made of the same material, but it doesn't have to be. Because the wall space it covers is usually small, you can get away with making a strong design statement in this area. Highly textured wallcoverings, such as cork or grass cloth, unpainted or rough-sawn wood, and textured paint are too hard to clean or are too delicate for a backsplash.

The most popular material for a backsplash is ceramic tile because it is both decorative and durable. Here you can indulge yourself in hand-painted tiles that would be too fragile for the countertop.

Laminate is effective only with a countertop of the same material. Likewise, stone and solid-surface backsplashes are generally used only with a countertop of the same material. Use stainless steel in gourmet-theme kitchens. Use mirror in small kitchens to give the illusion of depth in the room. Paint used on the backsplash should be gloss latex or alkyd; any wallcovering should be scrubbable or protected by a clear acrylic sheet.

The backsplash height is a design consideration. The continuous horizontal line of a short backsplash can draw together various kitchen design elements. Coordinate its height with that of windowsills, wainscoting, chair rails, and other kitchen features. Extending the backsplash to the bottom of wall cabinets gives the area a cohesive look, eliminates the need to paint that small awkward space, and facilitates cleaning.

The backsplash can become a functional storage element, as well. Frame a backsplash out from the wall several inches to form a ledge on which you can set plants, spice jars, or small appliances. Recess a box between studs in the backsplash, build shelves, and finish it for spice or utensil storage or an appliance garage. Cut slots into the ledge to store knives safely and within reach.

Edge Treatments

Some countertop edges are an integral part of the countertop surface, such as the curved edge of post-formed laminate; others are an applied piece of the same material, such as the V-caps edging ceramic tile. The edges of most countertops are built up by adding a support strip along the bottom for the edging material, giving the illusion of a thicker, more substantial surface.

Stunning effects can be achieved by using a contrasting material to edge a countertop. Wood trim adds a note of warmth to laminate, tile, and SSM countertops. Wood edging can be shaped with a router if a rounded edge is desired. To tie several different countertop materials together, use the same edge treatment.

Measuring Countertops

Cabinets, appliances, and countertops must fit the kitchen—and each other—like pieces in a giant jigsaw puzzle; therefore, even countertop dimensions are standardized. A

Contrasting the countertop and backsplash materials can be very effective as in this kitchen, where laminate countertops are backed by ceramic tile. The accent tiles replicate a Native American design, which fits the southwestern theme of the kitchen.

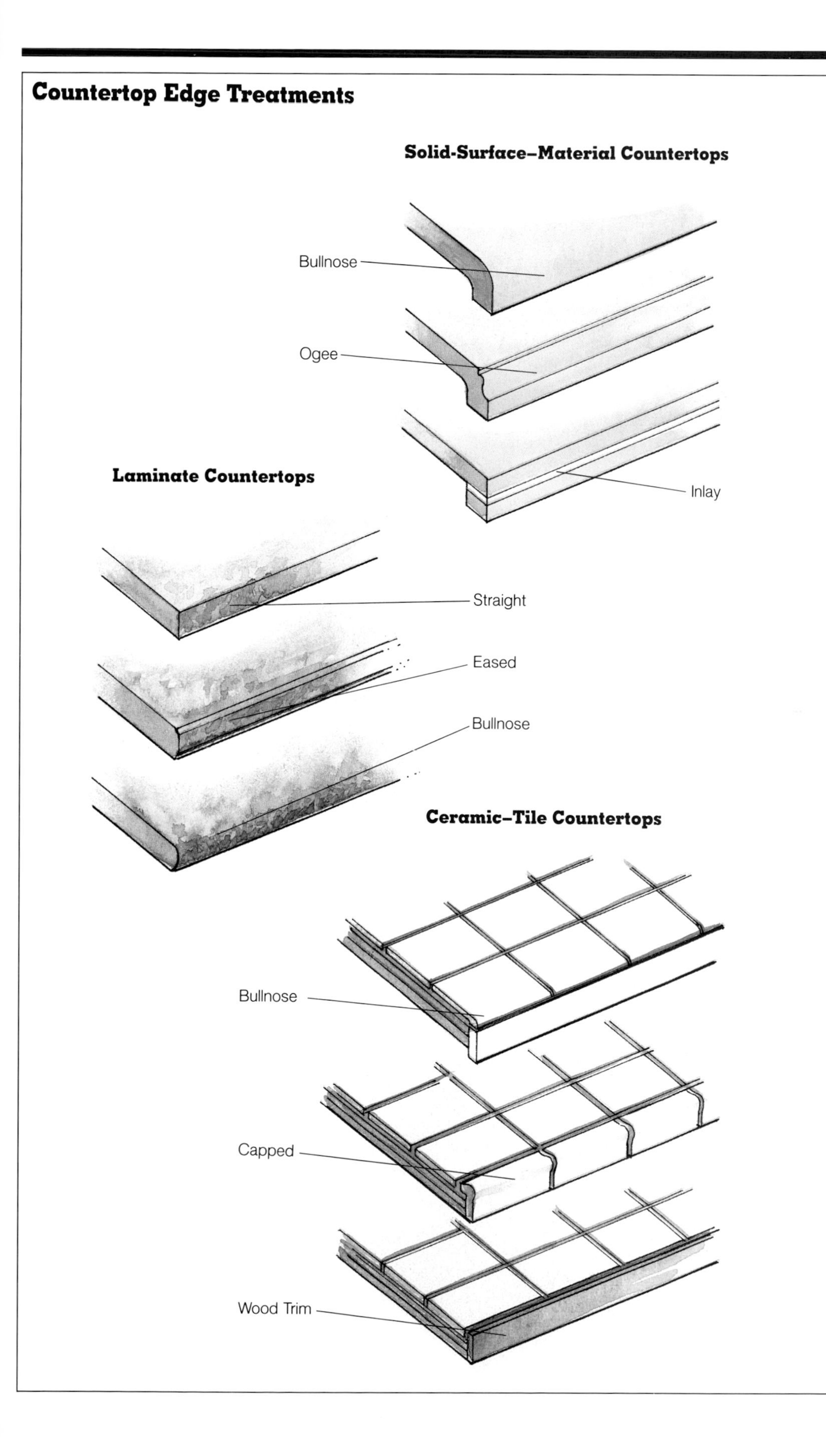

countertop is 25 inches deep, including the backsplash. This allows for a 1-inch overhang at the front and open ends of framed cabinets, ½ inch or less for frameless cabinets with ½-inch or thicker doors. The overhang where the countertop meets an appliance is ⅛ inch. Normal countertop height is 36 inches, but this can be customized by adjusting the height of the cabinets or other supports. The best general-purpose height for an individual is 2 to 3 inches below the elbow; for baking, 5 inches. When measuring countertop-material depth, allow for whether the backsplash will be attached on top of the countertop or behind it. For countertop length, take wall-to-wall measurements in several places and cut according to the longest result.

In calculating precisely for tiles, be sure to include the width of the grout lines. Some tile pieces will need to be cut, especially around curves or along angles.

For safety and convenience, minimum counter widths are required around appliances. Allow 12 inches between a side wall and a gas cooktop, 9 inches for an electric cooktop, and 3 inches for an undercounter appliance. There should also be 12 inches between a range or cooktop and a door. Allow 24 inches between a dishwasher and a counter at a right angle to it, 12 inches between a dishwasher and an angled corner sink. There should be 12 inches of counter between the sink and refrigerator, and between the sink and a right-angled counter. For an island or peninsula with a cooktop, allow a counter depth of at least 31 inches.

SINKS AND FAUCETS

Homely and utilitarian for years, the kitchen sink has blossomed into a design focal point, with colorful finishes, futuristic shapes, and versatile accessories. Because the sink is the center of kitchen activity, time invested in evaluating different style and function combinations is well spent.

Choosing Sinks

Sink manufacturers have paid close attention to the many uses their product has in the kitchen. The result is a wide array of sink sizes, shapes, and specialized designs for every function.

Make the following determinations before choosing a sink:

- How you use your sink
- The size and configuration that suits your needs
- The mounting method that best suits your countertop
- The material and finish that fit your design concept

If you can't think of one design that would suit all your needs, consider installing two sinks, especially if you are planning a laundry area or bar.

When choosing a sink, especially a large or unusual style, look at a sample, or a similar sink, to ensure that it suits both you and the space you've planned for it. Reach into the bowl to make sure its depth is comfortable; reach forward to check that the faucet position is convenient.

Before ordering the sink, you must first choose accessories and faucet and valve configurations (see page 87). Most sinks come with predrilled holes for accessory installation. While unused holes can be plugged, adding additional ones is often impossible. Because the sink is only a part of the cleanup center, it's important to coordinate the new sink with the dishwasher and drain choices (see page 90), disposers (see page 92), and trash and recycling bins (see page 93) in order to maximize the usefulness of the sink and the cleanup center as a whole.

Bowl Configurations

A kitchen sink may have one, two, or three bowls of various sizes and shapes, though they are usually rectangular. Bowl depths range from 6 to 15 inches; 7 inches is typical. For general chores, a shallow bowl is easier to reach into. A deeper bowl is better for washing large items, filling tall containers, and preventing splashes from messy jobs. Most sinks measure 22 inches front to back, to fit a standard countertop. They have a typical 3½-inch drain hole that can accommodate a garbage disposer. Some sinks have an integral dish-draining surface, called a deck, on either side or on both sides. In sink dimensions, the width in inches is stated first, followed by the measurement front to back.

Standard Single Bowl

This most-common sink measures 25 by 22 inches, although models may be as small as 15 inches front to back, or up to

The sink is often the hub of kitchen activity centers. Make it the visual focal point as well, by choosing a high-contrast color unit in the manner of this red knockout.

33 inches wide. A secondary version, often called a bar sink, comes as small as 12 by 15 inches rectangular or 15-inch diameter round, with a 2-inch drain hole. Some small sinks are available with a 15-inch-deep bowl.

Double-Bowl Sink

The most popular configuration, a double-bowl sink allows you to do food preparation and cleanup at the same time. Typically 33 by 22 inches, it may measure up to 48 inches wide. One of the bowls is normally fitted with a disposer. The bowls may be the same size, but often the disposer bowl is smaller and shallower.

Triple-Bowl Sink

This type of sink configuration has two typical bowls with a small, shallow disposer bowl in between. A standard triple-bowl sink measures 43 by 22 inches, but may be 60 inches wide or more. You can mimic the triple-bowl effect, and achieve the exact configuration you desire, by combining a standard sink and a small double sink to your own specifications.

Corner Sink

Also called a butterfly sink, an L-shaped sink designed for a corner has two bowls set at right angles to each other, and the faucet positioned between them. It may have a shallow disposer bowl in the center. If your countertops are short, the corner sink can free them up by occupying otherwise wasted corner space. Since the two bowls are not side by side, however, transferring wet items from one bowl to another can cause drips on the floor or countertop.

Designer Sinks

Also known as European sinks, designer sinks come in avant-garde shapes and styles. A typical example is a double sink with round, half-round, or oval bowls. Another configuration combines a small hexagon-shaped bowl and a large rectangular bowl. Such a sink adds a touch of excitement to the kitchen, and makes even a modest room look more upscale. But try out a designer sink in the showroom before you buy one. An unusual shape can be hard to work with; square pans and conventional sink accessories may not fit it. You also lose countertop space when using a designer sink: A 15-inch round bowl holds less than a 15-inch square bowl, while taking up virtually the same space.

When well designed, manufactured materials can be effective in even a traditional kitchen with a country theme. Here a double-bowl stainless steel sink has a self-rim mount that has been installed over a solid-surface–material countertop.

Plan the sink location, size, and mounting method prior to ordering countertop materials because each decision will affect the others. The yellow sink (above) has a self-rim mount that sits on top of the slab countertop. The recessed sink (below) is installed from below and held in place with clips attached to the underside of the countertop. Note the stripe around the sink that matches the countertop edging material.

Mounting Methods

The rim of the sink meets the countertop in one of several ways: with a self-rim, surface-mounted, flush-mounted, recessed, or undermounted. The sink may also be part of an integrally cast unit. The method you plan to use must be specified when you order the sink.

Each mounting method has a different look; choose the one that best fits the countertop material. A self-rimming sink has a lip that fits over the countertop. The sink is simply dropped into the opening. A bead of caulk under the lip seals it, and several clamps under the countertop secure it.

A surface-mounted sink has an edge that fits within the opening, flush with the surface of the countertop. A flat metal rim seals the joint, and clips underneath it hold the rim and the sink in place.

A flush-mounted sink—often used with a tile countertop—also fits within the opening but rather than sealing with a metal rim, the joint is grouted.

A recessed sink fits within the opening below the countertop surface. It is held in place by clips, or set on a rabbeted edge cut into the opening. This mount is used most often with ceramic-tile countertops; a cove-tile edging finishes the joint. With an undermounted sink, the joint is caulked. Both of these styles can be used with solid-surface–material countertops. Stainless steel sinks are not recommended for these mounts if the countertop is tile, because steel expands and contracts more than tile.

Integral sinks are made from the same material as the countertop. The most common is solid-surface material.

Materials

Choose a sink material based on the look you want for your kitchen, the upkeep you are willing to do, and, of course, your budget. All materials vary in quality; check the specifications and the manufacturer's warranty.

Stainless Steel

Preferred by the great majority of homeowners, a stainless steel sink is light, durable, and inexpensive. It is easier to bore additional accessory holes in stainless than in other materials, and it has a slightly flexible, forgiving surface if items are dropped into it. Steel with a gauge—or thickness—of 20 is adequate; the thicker 18 gauge is stronger and quieter, the 22 gauge sounds tinny and can dent. A high nickel content in the steel helps prevent corrosion, and a high chrome content improves the finish—get the highest of both that you can afford. A brushed finish hides scratches and water spots, while a mirror finish emphasizes them. Stainless steel sinks are available with an undercoating that muffles the din of the disposer and splashing water.

Enameled Steel and Iron

Enamel is a porcelainlike synthetic coating that is smooth and easy to clean (though abrasives should never be used). High-quality enamel resists chipping and staining. The traditional enameled cast-iron sink is heavy, durable, and expensive. Accessory holes are drilled before coating. An enameled steel sink is lighter and cheaper, but may have a less-durable finish. Enameled sinks come in dozens of rich colors from pastel to bold, and can be a dramatic focal point in your kitchen. Depending on the style, they can fit any kitchen decor.

Solid-Surface Material

Made of the same dense substance used for countertops, a solid-surface–material sink has stain and chemical resistance, repairability, and beauty unmatched by other products, making it an excellent, though very expensive, choice. A top-of-the-line SSM sink is molded in one piece with the countertop, forming a sleek, seamless, and easy-to-clean surface. Separate sinks made of SSM can be top-mounted, flush-mounted, or undermounted. Accessory holes can be drilled through the SSM.

Light Composites

Sinks composed of various materials such as resin, ground quartz, acrylic, or silica are the newest innovation to hit the market. Some composites are color constant throughout, others have a coating over another material. They have many of the same attributes as SSM sinks, are very expensive, but as yet do not come in a wide variety of colors or styles. Most have a thin flange for an overmount, fitting well into existing sink spaces.

Designer Materials

Sinks are also made from brass, copper, cultured marble, and specially glazed or painted ceramic. These are delicate and require diligent maintenance. They are recommended only as small accessory sinks in an entertaining center.

Faucets and Valves

Certainly functional, faucets and valves have become a design accent as well. The faucet is the pipe through which water flows into the sink. The valve or valves are the mechanism by which water is turned on and off.

The standard system has a spout plus separate valves for hot and cold water; the valves can be fitted with a variety of handles for easier adjustment and different styling. The standard system requires three holes in the sink deck. The single-handle, or mixer, valve allows one-hand temperature and volume control and requires only one hole in the sink deck. Standard faucet valves tend to last longer and are easier to maintain than mixer valves. Handles may be made of chrome, brass, wood, or porcelain, and many are enamel coated in fashion colors.

There is almost no limit to the faucet styles available. A rinsing faucet has a stem that can be pulled up for filling tall containers. The gooseneck style of a high-arc faucet serves the same purpose and has an attractive flair as well.

Most faucets are brass with a chrome finish. Less-expensive faucets may have chromed plastic parts, which do not hold up as well as all-metal versions. Plain brass faucets are making an elegant comeback, and copper and nickel finishes are also available. Uncoated brass faucets require regular polishing. The latest design trend, faucets enameled in vivid colors—often finished to match the sink—make an exciting accent.

Be sure to test faucets, valves, and handles in the showroom prior to purchase. The style you think looks best may not be the best choice for your kitchen—especially if you have trouble using your hands. Remember all the people who need to use the sink before deciding. Consider how convenient the handles are to reach and operate, how easy it is to move large items under the faucet, and how well the valves adjust water flow and control temperature.

Decide on the style of faucet and valves before ordering the sink, because the installation holes are factory-made and usually cannot be changed. The common number of holes is

If your plan calls for a secondary sink, consider a different faucet than for the main sink to fulfill different activity needs. The faucet for the primary sink includes a detachable sprayer, which makes dish rinsing easier. This second faucet is a tall gooseneck model designed for filling large pots and vases.

three or four, although some contemporary stainless steel sinks come with only one for a single-lever mixer faucet. Extra holes can be used for accessories, such as a soap dispenser, or filled with plugs. Some sinks do not have a rear deck for a faucet; in this case, the holes are made in the countertop.

Sink Accessories

An increasing variety of convenience gadgets are made for the cleanup area. Like the faucet, several accessories can be installed through holes in the sink ledge, and they must be specified before you order the sink. Any of these can also be installed through the countertop. Accessories include a hose sprayer, dishwasher air gap (sometimes required by code), water purifier, or dispensers for detergent, lotion, and instant hot water. The water accessories will require simple plumbing connections; in addition, the hot-water dispenser requires an electrical outlet. Water purifiers are available for installation under the sink.

Sink manufacturers offer a number of custom-fit food-preparation accessories. A cutting board provides an extra work surface; other items available include a colander and a draining basket.

Measuring Sinks

For a sink, allow at least a 1½-inch setback at the front edge of the countertop, but no more than 3 to 4 inches.

You'll need room behind the sink for faucet clearance. Leave at least 12 inches of countertop on one side of the sink and at least 24 inches on the other. Follow the manufacturer's instructions for what size to cut the countertop opening; this involves tracing the outline of the sink or a template onto the countertop.

If you want a sink-front bin, be sure to allow clearance for that as well.

Check local codes before choosing sink accessories. Some codes disallow a hose sprayer, for example, in order to save water. Others require dishwasher air gaps—seen here on the deck of the island sink—for sanitary efficiency.

Avoiding Common Placement Problems

Use the measurements on the manufacturer's specification sheets—not advertising brochures—for dimensions and door clearances. Common location-oriented problems can be avoided by using the techniques described here.

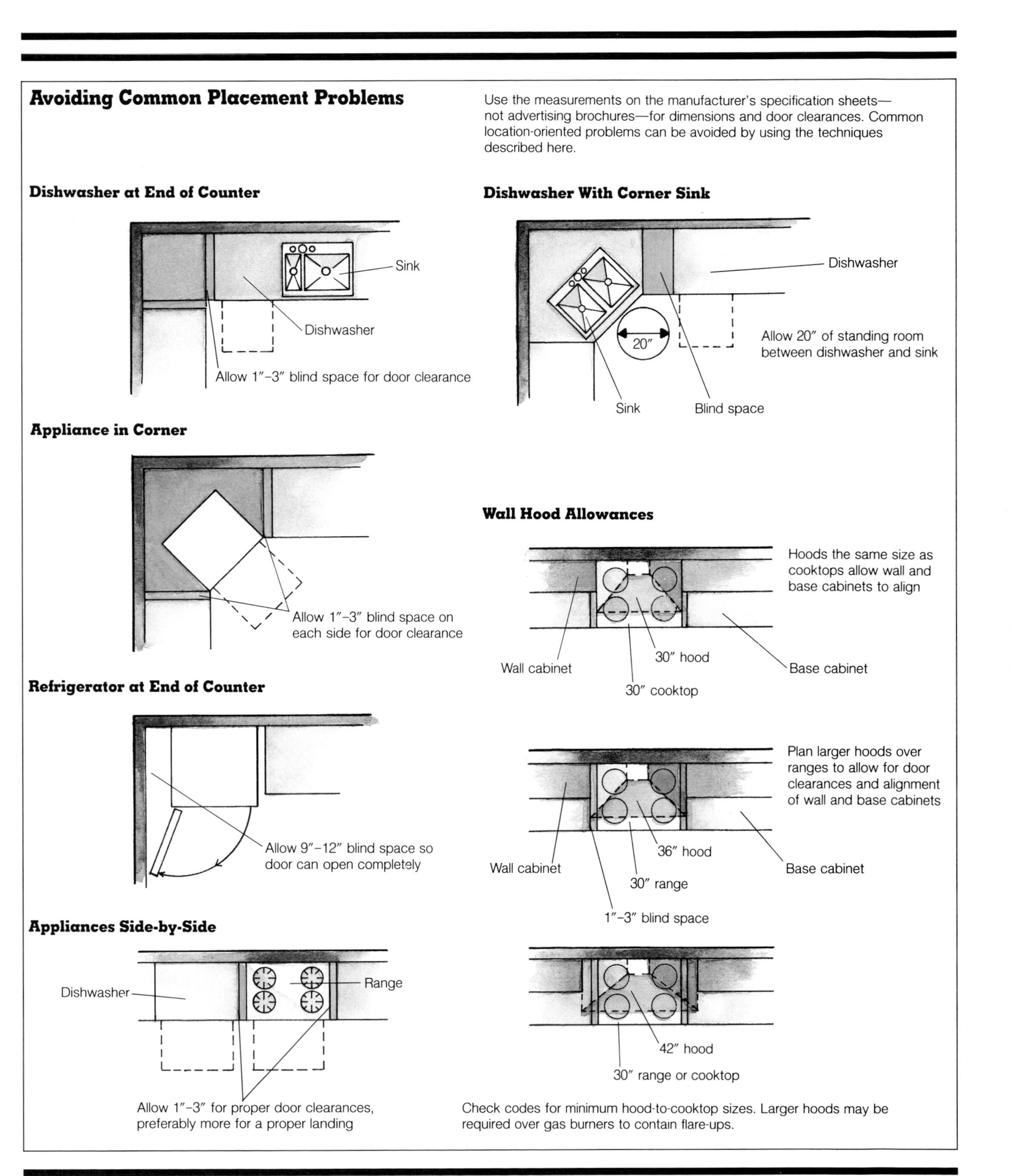

DISHWASHERS AND DISH DRAINS

Once considered a luxury, the dishwasher is now standard equipment in all modern kitchens. Energy-efficient models use less water than washing by hand, and a setting required on all machines allows dishes to air dry without using the electric heating element.

Choosing Dishwashers

As with all major appliances, when purchasing a dishwasher you need to balance style and quality with cost. Check machine styles and features; be especially concerned with capacity, durability, energy efficiency, and sound insulation.

The capacity of a dishwasher should be at least a meal's worth of dishes; for maximum energy efficiency it will hold a day's worth, so that you need run it only once in the evening. Capacity is determined not just by size, but by rack configuration. Check display models for a flexible arrangement that fits the type of dishes you normally use, whether roasting pans, cookie sheets, or goblets. Look for racks that are removable or adjustable. If your family is large or you entertain a lot, consider installing two dishwashers.

Installing a front panel on the dishwasher to match the surrounding cabinets produces a cohesive design line, which is perfectly suited to this modern kitchen.

The durability of a dishwasher is relative. A single person may use a dishwasher a hundred times in a year; a large family, a thousand times or more. Not everyone needs top-of-the-line quality. Check the warranty and consult the dealer about which model best matches your needs and your budget.

Given both the ecological and economical benefits of conserving fuel, energy efficiency is a definite plus in any major appliance. Is the new dishwasher officially rated for energy efficiency? Does it have a built-in water heater, allowing the house water heater to be turned down? Does it have an automatic air-drying cycle?

The sound insulation of the dishwasher will affect the comfort level of the kitchen and surrounding rooms. Noise levels range widely. If you plan to work or entertain in the kitchen while running the dishwasher, choose the quietest model possible. This can be difficult to check in the store; listen to friends' machines, and consult a consumer rating magazine.

Machine Styles

Portable dishwashers roll up to the sink and connect to the faucet. These are inconvenient to use; a remodeled kitchen should have a built-in dishwasher. If you already own a sound portable, you may be able to install it as a built-in using a conversion kit; ask the manufacturer whether your model is convertible.

Standard built-in dishwashers measure 24 inches wide, 24 inches deep, and 34½ inches high. They fit under the countertop and open from the front. They differ mainly in the features they offer.

A compact dishwasher, suitable for a small family or as part of a bar, is only 18 inches wide. An under-sink dishwasher, installed with a particular shallow sink, concentrates cleanup chores into a smaller area.

Dishwasher doors are either finished to match other major appliances or designed to be fitted with a front panel that matches the cabinets.

Features

Interiors are made of plastic, porcelain on steel, or stainless steel. Washing mechanisms are one or two rotating wash arms, or one arm with two levels. A floor strainer collects food; some models have a self-cleaning filter, or even a disposer, so that hand-rinsing of dishes is not necessary, although dishes must be scraped. An electric heating element, sometimes with a fan, dries the dishes.

A variety of automatic cleaning cycles allows you to personalize your dishwashing methods but avoid paying for features you won't use. Controls are dials, push buttons, or a touch pad; the latter is the easiest to wipe clean. The door lock and operation switches should be easy for you to use and read.

Placement

Figure out on which side of the sink you want to locate the dishwasher by considering both the available space and the way you prefer to wash dishes. In general, right-handed people will want the dishwasher to the right of the sink and left-handed people will want it on the left. Also consider the dishwasher in proximity to where dishes and flatware will be stored. The standard dishwasher is positioned next to the sink, although it can be up to 6 feet away.

The dishwasher needs its own electrical receptacle and in the majority of cases its own circuit as well—consult local codes. Its double receptacle may be shared with the disposer. Most codes require an air gap to prevent back-siphoning; this is mounted on the sink ledge or countertop. The dishwasher drain hose runs through the air gap to the disposer.

For a corner sink, allow at least a 12-inch clearance so you can stand at the sink with the dishwasher open. Allow 24 inches between the dishwasher and a corner cabinet. Avoid positioning it next to the refrigerator, since it radiates heat. If that is the only place available, add insulation between the two appliances.

A dishwasher may be mounted a foot or two above floor level to accommodate people who cannot bend over. A modified tall cabinet provides a sufficient installation. Support the machine with a framework of 2 by 4s.

Dish Drains

Most people still hand-wash some dishes, but with counter space at a premium, it can be difficult to drain them. Suspended over the sink, a wall cabinet or shelf that drains dishes can free up the counter and double as a storage rack. Popular in Europe, drying cabinets have slotted wood shelves and may or may not have doors. They are available in a few imported cabinet lines, or you can make your own by modifying an existing cabinet.

Another built-in drainage idea is a rack made from wood dowels or vinyl-clad shelving located above the sink. Wet dishes are placed on the rack, and the water drips back into the sink. In any case, be sure to plan a location for drainage near each sink.

When planning a dishwasher located within an island cleanup center, be sure to incorporate power needs, including a convenient location for the on-off switch, and to account for enough aisle room for traffic even when the dishwasher door is open. *Another view of this kitchen appears on page 29.*

WASTE-MANAGEMENT COMPONENTS

Local regulations may require that refuse be separated for collection and recycling. Health-conscious cooks and gardeners have rediscovered the benefits of composting. Thus, the lowly kitchen garbage can must be replaced by a waste-management system that handles all these needs efficiently and discreetly.

Garbage Cans

The kitchen stays tidier if waste receptacles are convenient. Plan space for small wastebaskets under the sink, at the communications center, near cutting boards, in the laundry room, and at the bar. Some cabinet manufacturers produce pull-out or tilt-out garbage bins as part of a cabinet line; the drawer or door fronts match the other cabinets. A plastic liner inside each bin can be removed for emptying and rinsing.

Trash Compactors

A trash compactor employs a rammer that crushes refuse into a compressed cube—about one quarter of its original volume. It should be used only for dry trash, such as paper, boxes, bottles, and cans. Since these materials should be separated and recycled, the usefulness of the compactor is limited. In addition, compacting trash inhibits its natural breakdown, slowing landfill decomposition. But, a compactor can be a convenient energy saver for large or rural households that must transport their trash to the dump.

A typical trash compactor is 15 inches wide and fits under the countertop. Some models are 12 or 18 inches wide, and freestanding or convertible models are also made. Most compactors use specially lined bags; some use grocery sacks. Features to look for include a foot pedal for opening the drawer when your hands are full, and a key-operated switch and lock to protect curious children. Most compactors have a deodorant dispenser, others a charcoal filter. A removable rammer simplifies cleaning, and a bag caddy with handles makes it easier to lift out a loaded bag. Look for an antijam rammer mechanism and effective sound insulation.

Install the compactor near the sink in the cleanup or food-preparation center. It requires a 120-volt electrical receptacle.

Disposers

Most kitchens today boast this handy little cleaner-upper. All standard sink drains are designed to accept a disposer. However, some areas of the country do not permit them and some septic tanks cannot accommodate them. On the other hand, some localities require disposers; refer to local codes. If you prefer to compost your food scraps, a disposer may not be necessary.

The disposer fits between the sink drain and the drain pipe. It requires an electrical receptacle and minor plumbing connections. A disposer operates either as a batch-feed, which runs only when the lid is locked into the drain opening; or as a continuous-feed, controlled by a switch, which allows you to add waste while the machine is running.

A quality disposer has a ½- or ¾-horsepower motor, stainless steel interior parts, and sound insulation. Look for overload protection and an antijam design, as well as a dependable warranty.

Consider both convenience and safety when planning the location of the on-off switch,

A trash compactor, seen here to the left of the sink, is a common element of a coordinated waste-management system. Matching the compactor to the dishwasher presents a coordinated look as well.

especially on an island sink; try placing the switch inside a cupboard. To prevent accidental disposer ignition, always a possibility with a continuous-feed disposer, install a batch-feed model at the onset.

Recycling

The heart of waste management in the modern kitchen is the recycling area. The art of efficient household recycling is still being developed, so design your system based on local regulations and your family's life-style. Because recycling started as a grass-roots movement, you will find up-to-date ideas for kitchen waste management through community action groups. Recycling consists of separating reusable solid waste from that destined for landfill, and composting food and other biodegradable waste for use in the garden.

Storage Bins

Plan an individual bin for each material that is to separated for collection. Many cabinet companies have heeded the call for convenient, attractive storage for recyclables. Commonly offered is an 18-inch-wide base cabinet with a pull-out drawer containing a pair of plastic bins. Most families will need at least two of these cabinets, side by side. Nonrecyclable trash may also be deposited in one of these bins. Because recyclables should be clean and dry, the bins do not need lids. Drawers designed to hold stacks of newspaper are also available. Don't forget a drawer for a can crusher, label stripper, binding twine, trash bags, and other relevant supplies.

If your local collector provides standard recycling bins, you may wish to order a specially designed base cabinet in which to keep them. Grocery bags measure 7 by 11½ by 18 inches tall. A drawer 21 inches deep by 12 inches wide will hold three bags for sorting. Locate the storage area for recyclables near an exterior kitchen door.

Compost

Any solid food waste, with the exception of meat and fish, can be composted. A kitchen compost bin may be quite small, since it should be emptied every day to prevent vermin, mold, and odor. It should be made of stainless steel or sturdy plastic and located in the food-preparation area, next to the sink or cutting board.

As with recycling, you'll have to tailor composting to your personal needs. One useful method is to cut a hole in the countertop, through which scraps are scooped into a dishpan or bucket clipped to the underside. Another is to provide access to the compost bin from both the kitchen side and from the outdoors. The hole for kitchen access should be covered securely; an insert made of the countertop material works best. Another method is to fit the top drawer in a base cabinet with a stainless steel or plastic liner with a lid. When the drawer is opened, scraps can be wiped off the countertop into the drawer. At least one cabinet manufacturer offers a pull-out cutting board with a compost drawer underneath. A line of sinks is manufactured with a hole that empties into a pail beneath it. A compost collector does not have to be built-in. Any sturdy container with a snug lid will serve the purpose.

Compost should be removed to outside storage at least once a day to avoid odor and pests.

These homeowners never have to discuss who takes out the garbage. The clever waste-management component shown here features an above-sink trap door leading to a trash bin accessible from the outside. More of this kitchen is pictured on pages 104 and 105 and is featured in the floor plan on page 107.

COOKING APPLIANCES

Until a few decades ago, a large wood-burning stove was the heart of the kitchen; it was used for heating the room, making hot water, baking bread, and frying the morning eggs. Now, cooking is faster and more modular, with each function performed by a specially designed appliance.

Choosing Cooking Appliances

Several decisions need to be made prior to shopping for cooking appliances. The procedure is to first make the following determinations:

• The power alternatives available in your kitchen

• Whether you want to install a range or component cooking system

• The range, cooktop, and oven configuration that best suits your space, design concept, and cooking style

Power Alternatives

When choosing between gas and electric cooking appliances, consider fuel availability and cost in your area, the current utilities setup in your kitchen, and the cost of changing it. In some areas, either gas or electricity is the fuel of choice, due to availability and low cost. Although cooking appliances do not use a great amount of either fuel, some utility companies give discounts for an all-gas or all-electric home. If your home is not currently served by gas, you may not want the added expense of installing gas lines, or the unsightliness of a propane tank. Conversely, if all your present cooking appliances are gas, it may be prohibitive to upgrade service to the 240-volt, higher-amperage circuits required by an electric cooktop or oven. However, your first consideration will be your cooking preference. Most professional cooks swear by the fine control of gas cooktop burners, although electric ovens are most respected.

Gas

All gas appliances function by burning either natural gas or propane fuel. Natural gas flows from the supplier through the meter beside your home into a supply pipe that goes to one or more appliances. An exposed pipe may be copper; a hidden pipe must be steel to prevent accidental puncturing.

Gas consumption is measured by the utility company in British thermal units, or BTUs, generated in one hour. One BTU is the energy required to raise 1 pound of water 1° Fahrenheit. All major appliances are rated in BTUs and have a rating tag attached to them with all the necessary data listed on it.

The BTU rating of an appliance (that is, the volume of gas

Cupid oversees the activities at the gas cooktop in this fanciful kitchen, which is also pictured on page 81. The wood storage is for the working fireplace on the opposite side of the peninsula.

it uses to do its job) determines which diameter of supply pipe you need to install; a professional-style range may require one larger than the normal ¾-inch pipe. A shutoff valve must be located on the pipe near the appliance, usually within 3 feet. Some localities permit a flexible-hose hookup, which makes positioning the appliance easier.

All gas cooking appliances manufactured today have electronic ignition, so there is no pilot light, reducing cost and the indoor pollution caused by combustion. This means, however, that even gas appliances require a 120-volt electrical receptacle.

If there is no natural-gas service in your area, you need a propane-gas tank, which must be located outside the house. The supply pipe is similar to that for natural gas, but the appliance must have a different orifice, which can be installed using a conversion kit.

Gas burners have various BTU ratings. A rating of 9,000 to 12,000 BTUs is normal for a residential burner; a rating of 15,000 to 20,000 BTUs is found in commercial burners. Such a powerful burner is called a superburner. Some cooks find it convenient to install one superburner for boiling water quickly, or for sautéing.

Electric

Each electric cooking appliance (except a microwave oven) requires a service of 240 volts, at 30 to 50 amps. You must know where you intend to locate each appliance when indicating electrical needs on your final floor plan (see page 106). Electric cooking produces no combustion, making it preferable for allergy and asthma sufferers and for tightly sealed homes.

Components

In the same manner as putting together a component stereo system, arranging various cooking appliances allows you to choose the exact item to fit your needs. You can mix power sources and brands. Above all, you can locate each appliance where it best suits your design.

Ovens

Consider a separate oven as part of a component cooking system or to provide auxiliary capacity to a range. A wall oven, as opposed to the oven section of a range, can be installed in a tall cabinet, either singly or paired with another oven or a microwave. It can also be installed in a base cabinet, under a countertop or cooktop, where two ovens can be positioned side by side.

Plan oven controls to be at eye level. The controls on most ovens are rotary, but touch pads are increasingly available and are easiest to clean.

Since an oven is not tended often during cooking, it can be located outside the main cooking area. An open oven door extends about 20 inches. Do not locate an oven where the open door will block a doorway or other heavy-traffic area. Position an oven at least 6 inches from a side wall. Provide a 15-inch landing on one side for setting down hot food.

An induction cooktop, lowered here for convenience, offers the heating quality of gas without the fear of combustion. The glass burners magnetically heat metal only, while staying cool themselves, and the pots and pans then heat the food. A paper towel left on the functioning cooktop will not catch fire!

The vast majority of ovens are electric, though gas models are made. If you opt for gas, look for one with pilotless electronic ignition. Each electric oven requires a 240-volt receptacle; a gas oven requires only a 120-volt receptacle for the accessories unless it is self-cleaning, in which case it too requires 240 volts.

The typical wall oven is 27 inches wide, though 24-inch and 30-inch models are available. Most ovens are 24 inches deep and require a couple of inches of air space at the back for venting. A pair of ovens, stacked, measures 50 inches tall. The typical oven interior is 19 or 20 inches wide. When choosing an oven, check its inside and outside dimensions. According to one cookting expert, an increase in width of only 2 inches can make room for an extra dish on the oven rack. Extra insulation is more energy efficient and keeps the kitchen cooler, but it can reduce the interior size of the oven. However, you can add insulation yourself when installing the oven by including rigid fiberglass panels inside the cabinet and on the sides and top of the oven.

Ovens are finished to match other major appliances. Doors with a translucent area that serves as a window are gaining in popularity.

Balance special features between ease of use and your budget. Self-cleaning ovens use a special high-heat cycle to burn off food residue, leaving the oven spotless. When cleaning starts, the door locks automatically and cannot be opened until the oven cools. These ovens are very well insulated.

Continuous-cleaning ovens have a special coating that makes residue burn off gradually as you cook. This feature is not recommended; the oven is never fully clean, and the interior will be damaged if cleaned by hand.

Convection ovens have a fan that circulates hot air around the food while cooking. This can cook foods up to one-third faster, at a lower temperature. This type works best for roasting, baking, and browning, but has little effect on moist foods such as casseroles and vegetable dishes. Convection and microwave features are often combined in one oven: The microwave component cooks the food rapidly and then switches to convection to brown it (then again, you could just switch ovens). Other oven features include delayed cooking start, rapid preheat, meat thermometers, and rotisseries.

Cooktops

Burners set in countertops are a popular component of a modern cooking system. Cooktops are available in gas models, although electric cooktops are by far the most popular because of their ease of installation and variety of features. The most common configuration for either type is four burners, two in front and two in back. Other arrangements include six burners, five burners, two burners, a single burner, and four in-line burners. Specialty burners such as grills and griddles are also available. For cooks who like both gas and electric, units of both types can be installed.

Convertible cooktops offer a variety of specialty burners in a modular form. Grills, hobs, griddles, woks, and other cooking tools come as modules that snap in and out of the cooktop as needed. This saves counter space that would be required for permanent installation and makes the cooktop more versatile. Consider carefully how often you would use these features, and whether changing and storing them would be worthwhile. If you choose a convertible cooktop, allow cabinet space close to the cooktop for storing the modules.

The typical two-and-two cooktop measures 20 by 28 inches, although other sizes are available. Cooktops drop into a hole in the countertop and hang from the flange around its edge.

The controls are usually top-mounted, though some models have a separate control panel that can be mounted in the cabinet below the cooktop. All gas cooktops, and the better electric models, have infinite-range control; some have thermostatic control for setting a specific temperature. An electric cooktop requires a 240-volt receptacle; a gas cooktop requires a standard gas pipe with shutoff valve. Surface materials include stainless steel; enamel over steel in a range of colors; and glass-ceramic in black, white, and gray.

Electric burners come in four types: coil, solid disc, glass-ceramic (coil or halogen), and induction. Look for a

Individual burners can be aligned in different ways to best serve your needs. Four in-line and four in a square are the most common configurations. Here the back burners are offset from the front ones, which allows for large pots to be used without them overlapping the burners.

cooktop that has coils that snap out easily for replacement. Specialty coils include a dish-shaped wok burner and an extralarge burner for a canning pot. Drip pans under the coils require constant cleaning.

Solid-disc elements, called hobs, have electrical wires embedded in a cast-iron disc. This produces very even heat, with slow warm-up and cool-down times. Some cooks feel the heat is not intense enough for sautéing. Choose discs that have a sensor in the center that indicates when the disc is hot, to prevent burns. The smooth disc surface is easier to clean than the drip pan under a coil, but may discolor over time.

Glass-ceramic cooktops have conventional coil elements under a smooth ceramic surface. Early glass cooktops earned a poor reputation due to discoloring and inefficiency, but many of these problems have been solved. A pattern on the glass surface indicates burner location; the pattern changes color when heated, but the change fades long before the surface is actually cool. Glass-ceramic cooktops are not quite as energy efficient as those with exposed elements; some heat is lost to the glass, and the entire surface can become quite hot. But spills and boil-overs are a snap to clean up, and the look is very sleek.

Halogen cooktops look like glass-ceramic cooktops but the burner heat source is a tubular light bulb filled with halogen gas. The bulb gives off more heat than light; its glow indicates it's on. Halogen burners are more instantly controllable than electric elements, offering some of the cooking advantages of gas. The halogen enables the tungsten filament to last far longer than an ordinary light bulb.

Induction cooktops also have a glass-ceramic surface, but there the similarity ends. Under the cooktop are solid-state, electronic induction coils that produce a magnetic field. When ferromagnetic (iron or steel) cookware is placed over the burner, this field passes into the cookware and makes it hot, cooking the food. The cooktop itself remains cool. Nonferrous cookware does not produce heat nor do small items such as flatware. Induction offers very fine temperature control with cooking times approaching those of gas. Although induction cooktops are expensive, they are very energy efficient, produce no combustion emissions, present little fire hazard, and are relatively safe for children.

Cooking tiles are another type of induction-cooking burner. They come in individual ceramic or glass 12-inch squares that can be arranged in unconventional ways, such as around a corner, along an island, or side by side. The tiles are mounted flush with the countertop. Their controls, usually an electric touch pad, are powered by a separate unit, which can be mounted alongside the tiles or in a separate area, such as in a drawer or across an island.

Gas cooktops are the standard among gourmet cooks. The flame offers infinite control and instant on and off. Pilotless ignition eliminates the pilot light and saves gas. Typical gas cooktops have the four-burner configuration, although some have five, six, or eight burners. A griddle is commonly available. Single gas burners can be lined up in a row, or one can be used as an auxiliary burner.

Ranges

The original cooking appliance, a range is basically a cooktop and oven all in one. It is usually either all gas or all electric, though gas burners are available with electric ovens. There are four basic types of range: freestanding, slide-in, drop-in, and commercial. A freestanding range has finished sides so that it can be positioned anywhere in the kitchen, for example, at the end of the cabinets. It has four burners on top and one or more ovens—and often a broiler—below. A backsplash displays controls or accessories; controls may be at the front. Some ranges have an upper oven as well, which may be a microwave. Many professional cooks recommend against an upper oven because its underside collects grease, the ventilation system is usually inferior, and it can interfere with looking into and stirring tall pots on the burners.

Freestanding Range

The typical freestanding range is 30 inches wide, though there are widths of 24 and 36 inches as well. The cooking surface is 36 inches tall, to fit a standard countertop, and 27 inches deep, which means it will protrude past the fronts of the base cabinets, especially if it is installed with space behind for the power connection.

Slide-in Range

A built-in range, also called a slide-in, is similar to a freestanding model. It is of standard countertop height but has no side panels, so it must be installed between base cabinets. It is designed with raised edges, allowing a more snug fit between the countertop and surrounding cabinets.

Drop-in Range

A drop-in range is set into the run of cabinets and supported by the counter. Its front is flush with the cabinets, and the top has a flange that overlaps the countertop for a sleek, integral look. A typical installation puts a drawer below the oven for storing pots; this must be specified when ordering cabinets. There is no backsplash, and the controls are at the front or on top, making the drop-in suitable for an island. It is usually 30 inches wide. Remember that the drop-in range is not as deep as a countertop, so the opening for it must be cut to size after the countertop is installed.

Commercial Range

A professional, or commercial, range has an aggressively low-tech, powerful design that appeals to serious cooks and to anyone who believes in the axiom "Form follows function." A typical commercial range uses gas and has six large burners and an oversized oven. It may also have a grill or a griddle, which takes a while to sufficiently heat up. The burners are rated 15,000 to 20,000 BTUs, compared with 9,000 to 12,000 BTUs for a residential range. It is stainless steel, very heavy, and usually 33 to 36 inches deep. Before you consider this heavy equipment for your kitchen, learn all you can about its installation requirements—the manufacturer will offer specifications.

Typically, the model you choose must be approved for home installation by the manufacturer, the *American Gas Association,* and local codes. A professional range generates great amounts of heat. It requires a clearance from the walls and cabinets, and the floor and surfaces surrounding the range must be covered with tile or other fireproof material. Such a range may be too large to fit through a doorway, and its considerable weight may require extra bracing of the floor joists. Most commercial ranges require a larger-diameter gas supply pipe than a residential range. Codes may require an elaborate ventilating system with special grease filters and a built-in fire-extinguishing capability.

If a commercial range appeals to you based on style, there are several commercial-style ranges manufactured for home use. These provide the high-BTU burners and large capacity needed for gourmet cooking without the commercial installation requirements. Check the manufacturer's installation specifications to see whether a model is recommended for home use. You may find a happy medium between high-volume, gourmet needs and residential requirements.

Commercial-style ranges bring high-quality burners and oven capacity to the home kitchen without the safety requirements of true commercial ranges. Home gourmets have encouraged manufacturers to expand their product lines to include a variety of sizes and colors, like the blue enameled version shown here. This kitchen is also pictured on page 10.

Microwave Ovens

The microwave oven has redefined home cooking. With no muss or fuss, it makes a hot meal available almost instantly, any time of day. It produces no combustion and no heat, and plugs into a 120-volt electrical receptacle—preferably on its own circuit, although this is not required.

Microwave ovens range in size from less than a cubic foot, to the size of a standard oven. A typical midsized oven measures about 20 inches wide, 15 inches tall, and 15 inches deep; power ranges from 400 watts to 1,000 watts or more. The appropriate size and power for you will depend on how you plan to use the oven.

There are several ways to install a microwave oven for a built-in look. Consider mounting it in a specially designed microwave wall cabinet, which includes storage; on a shelf beneath a short wall cabinet with a full-length wall cabinet along each side; as the upper oven of a two-oven range; in an oven cabinet as the upper unit of a double wall oven; or hanging beneath the wall cabinets using a bracket designed especially for that purpose. If hanging the microwave, remember to allow at least 12 inches of space between the bottom of the oven and the counter. A shorter space renders the countertop below the oven useless, although it can be filled with a built-in drawer; this leaves the narrow strip of countertop in front of it unusable, however. The oven door typically opens on the right side, though some open downward like a conventional oven.

For convenient use, position the microwave oven so that its floor height is between the elbow and shoulder height of the average cook.

Plan on cabinet storage near the microwave oven for the particular cookware it requires. Allow a 15-inch landing on one side for setting down items hot from the oven.

Deciding on the best cooking system for your kitchen depends on your cooking style and the space requirements of the room. A range, like the blue commercial-style one above, is the more traditional choice, but a component system (below) will suit even the most traditional kitchen, when as well designed as it is here.

VENTILATION

The kitchen ventilating system is a major appliance, as important as any other, and must be chosen with great care. Proper ventilation keeps kitchen surfaces free of grease and rids the air of fumes, steam, and odors.

Determining Need

The system that works best for you depends on the size of your kitchen and the location of the cooktop. Where you position the cooktop will depend in part on the ease of running ventilating duct work to the outside.

Kitchen air should be exchanged every four minutes. The ability of an exhaust fan to move air to the outside is rated in cubic feet per minute, or CFM. To figure the CFM capacity needed for the kitchen exhaust fan, multiply the square footage of the room by two. For example, a kitchen 10 feet by 12 feet would require a fan rated 10 times 12 times 2, or 240 CFM—more if the ceiling is higher than 8 feet. The minimum CFM capacity for a hooded fan over a cooktop is 40 times the width, in feet, of the hood (50 times if the hood is over an island or peninsula). For adequate kitchen ventilation, an auxiliary exhaust fan would also be needed. Do not overventilate, however. An overpowered exhaust fan can cause a backdraft in an airtight house, pulling in combustion fumes from the furnace, chimney, and hot-water heater, and radon gas from the foundation. It will also cause excessive loss of heated or air-conditioned indoor air.

Choosing Ventilating Systems

Often, ventilation is required by code, especially for indoor grills and gas cooktops. The code may dictate both the size and style of the ventilating system for your kitchen.

Hood/Vent

A hooded exhaust fan over the cooktop, ducted to the outside, provides the most efficient kitchen ventilation. The hood collects rising cooking fumes so the fan can remove them; the fan does not "pull" the fumes up. The depth of the hood, front to back, determines how far above the cooktop it may be placed: a 16-to-17-inch hood should be no more than 21 inches above the cooktop; an 18-to-21-inch hood, 24 inches; a 24-inch hood, 30 inches (which is the maximum for any hood). At minimum, the width of the hood should match the width of the cooktop (see page 89).

Fans

The two main types of fan are propeller style and squirrel-cage style. The cylindrical squirrel-cage fan is quieter and more powerful. The noise level of a fan is measured in sones. Choose a fan rated at 8 sones or less, and try to listen to a fan before you buy it—a noisy fan will not get much use. Often, the fan is built into a metal hood assembly that includes

Because of their size and central location, hoods over island cooktops are a major design element. If your floor plan calls for an island cooking center, such as this one, consider choosing a hood that matches the cabinets.

Downdraft Ventilation

The major alternative to a hooded exhaust fan is a downdraft ventilating system. Found in many cooktops, especially those with grills, this system has vents at the center, sides, or back of the cooktop through which a fan exhausts fumes downward through a duct. Downdraft ventilation can be effective under certain conditions: The fan must be on throughout the cooking process, and pans must not block the vent. A downdraft fan is more powerful than a hood fan, and can cause backdraft problems. Its ducting must follow the manufacturer's requirements to prevent strain on the motor, which can cause automatic shutoff.

Ducting

Proper ducting determines whether an exhaust fan can work to its rated capacity. The shortest, straightest duct is best; try to plan cooktop placement so that the fan can be ducted straight out an adjacent exterior wall or through the roof. The fan manufacturer will specify the maximum allowable duct length; keep in mind that each turn is valued as 10 feet of ducting, and the number of allowable turns is limited, typically to a total of 180 degrees. Duct size is also specified; this is usually 7 inches round or 3¼ by 10 inches rectangular (to fit between studs). A duct passing through an unheated area must be insulated. Where the duct exits the house, a vent called a wall cap, eave cap, or roof jack must be installed. These incorporate a backdraft damper and a bug screen.

Not all kitchen ventilation requires a ducted hood. An induction cooktop can be vented by a backsplash fan (above). For safety's sake openable windows should never be located above a cooktop but are ideally located over a sink (below).

a light and a removable filter, and may feature a warming lamp. It requires a 120-volt receptacle. The fan and filter may also be purchased separately, and the hood custom-built to match your decor. Some cabinet lines offer a unit that looks like a cabinet, but pulls out to form a ventilation hood.

Nonvented, or ductless, hoods have a fan that circulates air through a filter and then back into the room. A filter may help remove some grease, but it has no effect on heat, steam, or fumes. A ductless hood is not recommended except where ducting is impossible.

A wall or ceiling exhaust fan, ducted to the outside, can do an adequate job of exchanging the air in the kitchen, but it does not trap cooking fumes.

REFRIGERATORS AND FREEZERS

The electric refrigerator and freezer have done as much to change the family life-style as any technology of the twentieth century. By keeping food fresh for long periods of time, these appliances have revolutionized shopping patterns and purchasing power.

Choosing Refrigerators and Freezers

A refrigerator or freezer has a life span of 15 years, so consider carefully how your family's needs may change. A refrigerator can consume thousands of dollars in electricity in its lifetime. In fact, the refrigerator is one of the largest energy users in the house, so compare the energy-guide labels, required on all appliances, to find the most efficient model. Each refrigerator or freezer requires its own 120-volt receptacle and probably its own circuit, determined by code.

The procedure for choosing a new refrigerator and freezer begins by making the following determinations:

- Your cold-storage needs
- The machine type that best fits the space
- The interior features that best suit your cooking style
- The style that complements the look of your kitchen

Machine Types

Refrigerators are manufactured in a gamut of colors. Most enameled refrigerators have a textured finish that disguises smudges. Commercial and professional-style refrigerators are finished in stainless steel. Many have view-through glass doors—an incentive for neatness! There are also special doors for barrier-free design.

Some manufacturers produce door panels that match the cabinets, giving a built-in look. The hardware for attaching the panels, called a trim kit, is provided by the refrigerator manufacturer, and the panels by a cabinet manufacturer.

Single-Door

The single-door refrigerator is the smallest and least expensive. Most have a mini freezer compartment inside that must be defrosted manually. There are 36-inch-wide machines available that are refrigerator only, and these are handy for extra storage or paired with a separate freezer.

Two-Door

The two-door refrigerator/freezer has a separate freezer, usually at the top. Some models have a bottom freezer that rolls open, bin-style, providing easier access to both freezer and refrigerator, as well as efficient cold storage. This model may have a double refrigerator door, called a French-door refrigerator. The freezer maintains a temperature of approximately 0° F, cold enough for long-term storage. Most models have automatic defrost. This style comes in total capacities up to 24 cubic feet.

Side-by-Side

The side-by-side refrigerator/freezer has a refrigerator on the right and a freezer on the left. The narrower doors have a more compact swing, making this style ideal where space is tight. Children can reach the freezer easily. However, the deep, narrow shape of the interior makes food storage more difficult. Check to be sure that the occasional frozen pizza or holiday turkey will fit in the freezer. Countertop placement must allow the doors to open fully on both the right and the left in order to remove drawers and bins. All side-by-side models have automatic defrost. The freezer maintains a temperature of approximately 0° F. The total capacity is up to 30 cubic feet, with a relatively large freezer space. Some models have a small third door above the freezer compartment for often-used items.

Commercial

Commercial refrigerators are gaining popularity among cooks who want large capacity and no-nonsense design. They may have one or two compressors, which can be located on top of the refrigerator or even in a separate area. These compressors can be noisier than those designed for home use.

Under-counter

Small, under-counter refrigerators, typically 36 inches tall by 24 inches wide, are handy for extra storage and can be an excellent option for a bar, apartment add-on, or as an addition to your main refrigerator.

Combination cooktop–under-counter refrigerators and sink–under-counter refrigerators are available from several manufacturers. While these will not meet the needs of a family kitchen, they are wonderful space-saving devices for apartments, office kitchens, and for entertainment rooms that are some distance from the main kitchen. Check manufacturer specifications for plumbing and electrical needs, and local codes for ventilation requirements.

Separate Freezers

There are two types of separate freezers: upright and chest. Of the two, the upright offers easier access to its contents and takes up less floor space; its size and shape resemble a refrigerator. If you use a freezer on a daily basis, this type may be worked in to the kitchen design, depending on space allotments. An upright may have automatic defrost.

The chest freezer opens at the top. Due to its shape, it maintains cold more efficiently but, because of its bulkiness, is best installed in a garage, basement, or utility room. Most chest freezers are manual defrost. Meant for long-term storage, they aren't opened much, preventing rapid frost buildup. A chest freezer is 36 inches high, and ranges from 27 to 32 inches deep and 32 to 72 inches wide. Because their contents are often valuable, chest freezers usually have a keyed door and a light to indicate that power is on. Also look for a defrost drain, deep- and quick-freeze sections, an interior light, and sturdy rollers.

Interior Features

The interior design of a refrigerator determines how convenient the appliance is to use. Look for adjustable shelves; glass is sturdier than wire, and catches spills. Drawers and door shelves should be wide and deep enough to hold the intended food items. For easy cleaning, as many parts as possible should be removable, including door shelves that block drawer access. Controls should be readily accessible, and not in the way of the storage area. Finally, make sure the refrigerator has smooth, sturdy rollers so it can be moved for cleaning.

An ice maker is practical enough to be considered a basic feature, though it is usually an option you must purchase separately. When figuring cost, include installation of the copper water-supply tube.

Some features that seem like luxuries are actually energy savers. Door dispensers, for example, serve up crushed ice, chilled water, and juices without the need to open the refrigerator door. Some models have a small exterior compartment that can house milk cartons and soft drinks. One high-end refrigerator even makes ice cream and frozen yogurt.

Measuring Refrigerators and Freezers

Kitchen-design standards call for 10 to 12 cubic feet of interior refrigerator space for two people, plus 2 cubic feet for each additional person. Freezer space should be 2 cubic feet per person. The capacities claimed by manufacturers are not all usable space, however, so add 2 to 4 cubic feet to your estimate. Bigger is not always better. A refrigerator kept partially full uses more energy to cool.

To figure the placement of a refrigerator in your kitchen, measure the height, width, depth, airflow space requirements, and door swing.

The exterior of a full-sized refrigerator measures 24 to 60 inches wide and 58 to 72 inches tall. While some manufacturers make 24-inch-deep models to fit between cabinets, most refrigerators are 30 inches deep. The majority of modern refrigerators require just a 1-inch airflow space all around. Door swing ranges up to 35 inches out into the room, perhaps blocking traffic flow; the door must also have room to open wider than 90 degrees to make shelves and drawers accessible. There should be 15 inches of countertop on the latch side of the refrigerator.

The awkward depth of most refrigerators requires some design ingenuity to achieve a built-in look. The refrigerator can be boxed by panels that match the cabinets, with full-depth short cabinets above. If floor space is plentiful, the adjacent base cabinets can be pulled out flush with the front of the refrigerator, and the counter made deeper.

Upright freezers can be built in as well, but lack of variety in colors and trim panels for most models makes them harder to coordinate with the kitchen decor.

Appliances must accommodate everyone in the family. The narrow doors of a side-by-side refrigerator (above) are easy to open from a seated position, which is why it was chosen by a wheelchair user. Another view of this kitchen appears on page 13. The cold-storage requirements of a large family necessitate two refrigerators (below). Alternating the direction the doors open allows both appliances to share one landing.

GOOD FRIENDS
GREAT DINNERS

FINALIZING THE DESIGN

Turning dreams and ideas into working remodeling plans and trading your wish list for a shopping list of materials and fixtures is the final act of designing your new kitchen. In this chapter, you finalize your kitchen plan—tailoring all the previous information to your needs. Finally, take a look at some ideas to inspire your personal style, finishing touches that make the new kitchen truly yours.

The original floor plan for this kitchen appears on page 33. On the homeowners' remodeling wish list were increased light, better traffic flow, updated appliances, more storage, easier maintenance, and a modern style. Turn the page for a look at the final floor plan and see how they achieved their goals.

FINALIZING THE PLANS

Combine your best preliminary plan from the second chapter with the construction elements, cabinets, fixtures, and appliances you have chosen to produce the final plans.

Drawing the Final Plan

The final plan serves as a visual guide for the actual remodeling work. It shows in accurate detail the shape, size, and position of every element in the kitchen. Measurements for cabinets, fixtures, and appliances are the exact dimensions of the particular models you have chosen, based on the manufacturer's installation literature. Any prescribed clearances, such as those around a refrigerator or a corner cabinet, also appear on the plan. The positions of light fixtures, switches, and receptacles are detailed.

Draw the final plan using the same tools as before (see page 32), on graph paper or architect's vellum, gridded or plain, in sheets 18 inches by 24 inches. Use a pencil graded number 3 or harder. If the plan will be submitted to the building department—especially if structural changes to the house are involved—you probably need to have it finalized by an architect or professional designer. You can finalize the plan as outlined here and submit a clean, perfect copy for the designer's reference.

Trace the base plan—or the new floor plan, if you changed it—onto the vellum. Do not use a photocopy as the size may not be accurate. Using the preliminary plan as a guide, draw in every structural element of the new kitchen, noting its name and exact dimensions (within its outline, if possible; otherwise make a marginal note and direct a line to it).

Indicate door swing by drawing a curved line. Double-check that doors can swing unimpeded, that appliance doors have room to open fully, that aisles are wide enough, and that corner cabinets won't obstruct each other.

On the completed plan, write the legends: "Do not scale drawings. Measurements govern"; and "Verify all dimensions on the site. Notify (yourself or contractor) of any discrepancy." These mean that anyone using the plan must work by the measurements given, not by the way the drawings look, and that if the measurements don't jibe, someone in charge must be notified before work can proceed.

Drawing Specialty Plans

You may wish to make more-detailed drawings of certain elements of the kitchen design because the changes are complicated or in order to show structural changes to the building department or to a builder. To do this, trace a copy of the final plan, omitting measurements and other notations for clarity.

If ceiling elements are simple, they can be detailed as dotted lines on the floor plan; however, if the ceiling will be structurally changed, a specific ceiling plan may be required.

Other common specialty plans include those for electrical, plumbing, ventilation, and cabinets.

Details

Plans of small areas, called details, give a close-up view of a single aspect of the overall design. Commonly, details show the pattern on a tile installation or the profile of trim pieces on a cabinet door. These are drawn on a larger scale of your choice, such as 3 inches to 1 foot. By drawing such elements to scale before installation, you can see how they'll look, and installers can know exactly what you want them to do.

Sections

A cutaway view of a "slice" of the building showing a complicated construction element is called a section. It shows the builder cross-section details of a wall, for example, to show a wallboard-and-insulation fire barrier, or of the roof structure, if you are vaulting the kitchen ceiling. These section plans may be required by the building department, especially if you are planning exterior changes that affect the foundation of the house.

Elevations

An elevation is a two-dimensional scale drawing of a wall, with all its elements in place. Unlike plan drawings, elevations are fairly representational pictures of the features within the room. You don't need elevations for every project, but they are instrumental for complicated installations, for planning and ordering cabinets, and for checking the visual relationships between various features.

Elevations are drawn using the same tools and techniques as for a plan, in the same ½-inch scale. To produce an elevation, use the final plan, manufacturers' specifications, and photographs and illustrations of individual fixtures.

Do an individual elevation for each wall, as needed. Start by drawing the outline of one wall—it will most likely be a rectangle. Add the architectural details, such as windows and doors. Then plot the outlines of the major cabinets, such as a tall storage unit, sink unit, wall-oven unit, and corner units; remember to include the height of the toe kick.

Next, add the appliances, using the manufacturers' specifications. Then draw the counters; be sure to position them at the height you have chosen, and draw the countertop thickness and any overhang.

Draw all the walls this way. Draw all sides of any island or peninsula, too. Line up the drawings and check that they form a harmonious whole, with adequate storage, before making the final elevations. At this point, you can also sketch in any molding details and hardware styles you are considering. You can try various color schemes with colored pencils on photocopies. On the final elevations, write the name and dimensions of every element.

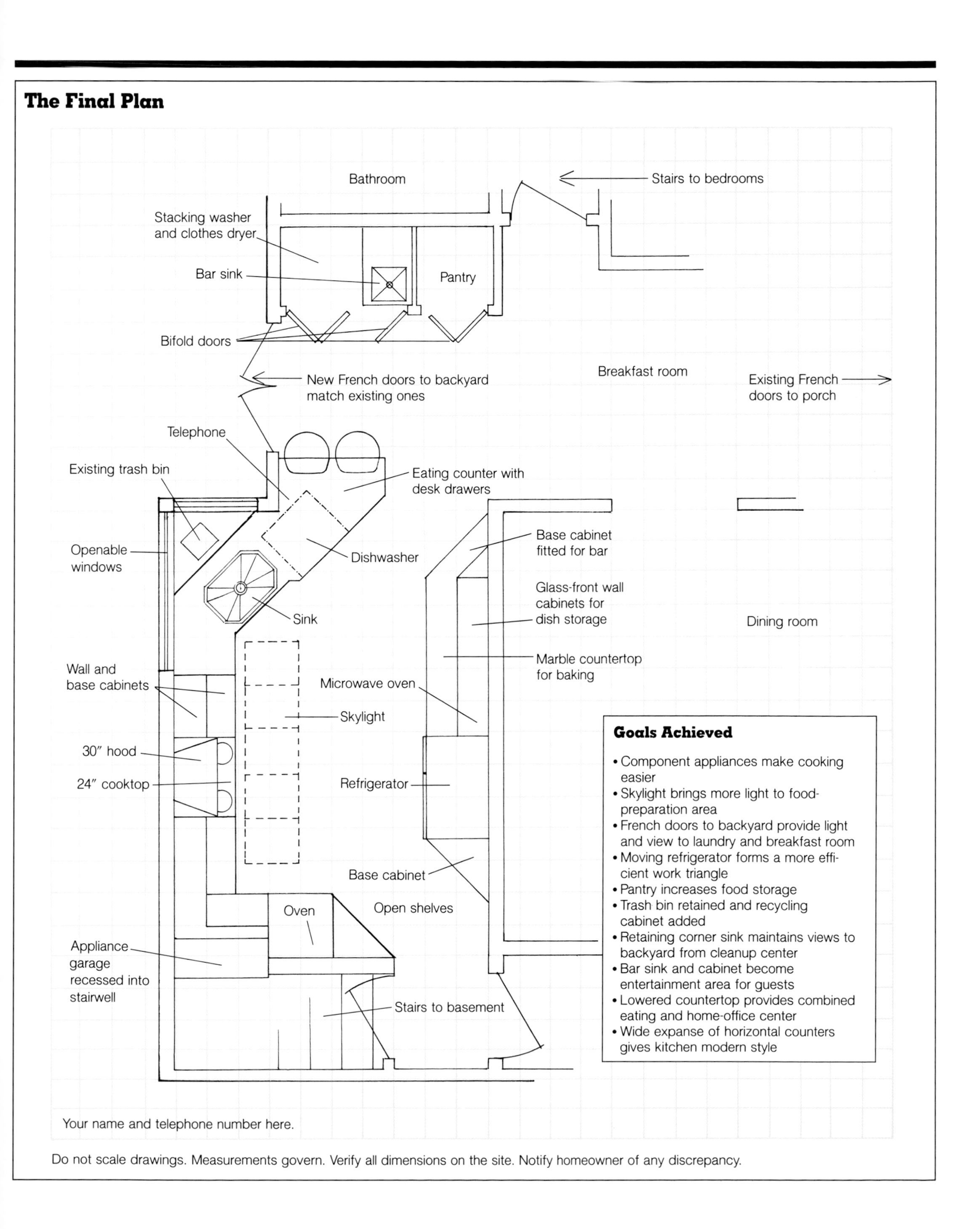
The Final Plan
Bathroom
Stairs to bedrooms
Stacking washer and clothes dryer
Bar sink
Pantry
Bifold doors
New French doors to backyard match existing ones
Breakfast room
Existing French doors to porch
Telephone
Existing trash bin
Eating counter with desk drawers
Openable windows
Dishwasher
Base cabinet fitted for bar
Glass-front wall cabinets for dish storage
Sink
Dining room
Wall and base cabinets
Microwave oven
Marble countertop for baking
Skylight
30″ hood
24″ cooktop
Refrigerator
Base cabinet
Oven
Open shelves
Appliance garage recessed into stairwell
Stairs to basement
Goals Achieved
• Component appliances make cooking easier
• Skylight brings more light to food-preparation area
• French doors to backyard provide light and view to laundry and breakfast room
• Moving refrigerator forms a more efficient work triangle
• Pantry increases food storage
• Trash bin retained and recycling cabinet added
• Retaining corner sink maintains views to backyard from cleanup center
• Bar sink and cabinet become entertainment area for guests
• Lowered countertop provides combined eating and home-office center
• Wide expanse of horizontal counters gives kitchen modern style
Your name and telephone number here.
Do not scale drawings. Measurements govern. Verify all dimensions on the site. Notify homeowner of any discrepancy.

ADDING FINISHING TOUCHES

Fashion magazines claim it is the accessories that make the outfit. The same can be said of accessorizing the kitchen. Once the floor plan is completed and construction begins, you can return to your wish list and start compiling the finishing touches for the room.

Window Treatments

Install window treatments to harmonize with the look of the house and the window, from both the inside and outside. Also consider the practicalities, such as covering the window against the elements and for privacy.

If the window admits strong sunlight at some part of the day, you will need filtering blinds, either vertical or horizontal, to cut the glare and to protect people and furnishings from ultraviolet rays.

Drapes in eating areas should be lined for extra protection against winter drafts. Floor-to-ceiling draperies around larger windows in an adjacent family or dining room can be matched with shorter-length curtains, tiebacks, or a valance for smaller kitchen windows.

Modes for hanging window treatments depend on the kitchen look. A plain rod, painted or stained and set on brackets, could support simple drape panels hung by tags or loops in a country kitchen. A classic kitchen might have a shirred valance over curtains pulled back with brass rosettes. A fold-down canvas panel or a brightly colored Roman shade mounted on dowels will smartly accent a black-and-white Eurotech kitchen.

Use window treatments to enhance a view. Where there is a fine view to be framed, plan drapes that pull back completely. If the window does not need to be covered, use a contrasting trim treatment to frame the view from a picture window the same way you use a mat when framing a picture. To block an unsightly view from the bottom of a window, use an upside-down window shade mounted on nautical hardware. To completely hide an unwanted view, hang a

Designers of the most successful kitchens plan finishing details before any construction begins. Here the white wrought-iron table and chair fit this breakfast nook perfectly because the built-in seating was planned to accommodate the furniture.

piece of stained glass that complements the kitchen colors, or find a stained-glass window to mount in the window frame.

Furniture

The tables, chairs, stools, buffets, serving tables, and fireplace settees in the kitchen must all harmonize with the design concept. A simple way to coordinate the room is to match wood furniture to the cabinets. Some manufacturers offer furniture pieces to match their cabinet lines; others will finish your own raw furniture if you are willing to pay the two-way freight to their factory on top of the finishing costs. You can, of course, paint or stain furniture to match the cabinets yourself.

Tie together various kitchen elements by using matching fabrics. If you sew, use the same fabric on window treatments and chair seat covers. Some wallcovering manufacturers produce matching or coordinating fabrics for curtains, shelf lining, and seat covers.

Art

Whether your tastes run to formal or fun, the same rules of scale, shape, pattern, texture, line, and color that apply to the room as a whole also apply to displays within it. Your choice of exhibits and art is obviously a matter of personal taste, but whatever you decide to display in your new kitchen should work with the style and theme. A collection or artwork might trigger or even establish the kitchen theme; the color in a piece of art might be the jumping-off place for the entire color scheme. If your art deco jukebox, life-sized sculpture, or neon sign requires power or plumbing, be sure to keep it in mind as you determine the floor plan.

Accessories

Even if your accessories aren't one of a kind, they should cohere with the look of the kitchen. For a formal, symmetrically balanced window wall, for example, evenly place same-sized potted plants on a shelf. For an asymmetrical room, use a row of candlesticks arranged from tallest to shortest. Repeat curvilinear lines with a round clock or mirror. Pick up the color of countertops in the mats of framed prints. Make a photo gallery in an alcove with frames stained to match the wood cabinets or painted to match the brightly colored drawer and cabinet pulls.

Remember linens, too, from placemats to pot holders, which need to be coordinated to the design concept. Notify friends and family of your color scheme so they can be sure to give you the right new accessories when you invite them to the warming celebration of your remodeled kitchen.

Continue to use the principles of design as you accessorize the new room. Matching kitchen accessories to the red diamond in the resilient tile floor uses the principle of color to coordinate the elements. Imagine how different this room would look if black was used as the accent color or if all the accessories were white.

NDEX

Page numbers in italic type indicate references to illustrations.

U.S./Metric Measure Conversion Chart

		Formulas for Exact Measures			Rounded Measures for Quick Reference		
	Symbol	When you know:	Multiply by:	To find:			
Mass (Weight)	oz	ounces	28.35	grams	1 oz		= 30 g
	lb	pounds	0.45	kilograms	4 oz		= 115 g
	g	grams	0.035	ounces	8 oz		= 225 g
	kg	kilograms	2.2	pounds	16 oz	= 1 lb	= 450 g
					32 oz	= 2 lb	= 900 g
					36 oz	= 2¼ lb	= 1000 g (1 kg)
Volume	tsp	teaspoons	5.0	milliliters	¼ tsp	= 1/24 oz	= 1 ml
	tbsp	tablespoons	15.0	milliliters	½ tsp	= 1/12 oz	= 2 ml
	fl oz	fluid ounces	29.57	milliliters	1 tsp	= 1/6 oz	= 5 ml
	c	cups	0.24	liters	1 tbsp	= ½ oz	= 15 ml
	pt	pints	0.47	liters	1 c	= 8 oz	= 250 ml
	qt	quarts	0.95	liters	2 c (1 pt)	= 16 oz	= 500 ml
	gal	gallons	3.785	liters	4 c (1 qt)	= 32 oz	= 1 liter
	ml	milliliters	0.034	fluid ounces	4 qt (1 gal)	= 128 oz	= 3¾ liter
Length	in.	inches	2.54	centimeters	⅜ in.	= 1 cm	
	ft	feet	30.48	centimeters	1 in.	= 2.5 cm	
	yd	yards	0.9144	meters	2 in.	= 5 cm	
	mi	miles	1.609	kilometers	2½ in.	= 6.5 cm	
	km	kilometers	0.621	miles	12 in. (1 ft)	= 30 cm	
	m	meters	1.094	yards	1 yd	= 90 cm	
	cm	centimeters	0.39	inches	100 ft	= 30 m	
					1 mi	= 1.6 km	
Temperature	° F	Fahrenheit	5/9 (after subtracting 32)	Celsius	32° F	= 0° C	
					68° F	= 20° C	
	° C	Celsius	9/5 (then add 32)	Fahrenheit	212° F	= 100° C	
Area	$in.^2$	square inches	6.452	square centimeters	1 $in.^2$	= 6.5 cm^2	
	ft^2	square feet	929.0	square centimeters	1 ft^2	= 930 cm^2	
	yd^2	square yards	8361.0	square centimeters	1 yd^2	= 8360 cm^2	
	a.	acres	0.4047	hectares	1 a.	= 4050 m^2	